Sandy Berger Should Be In Jail

Then they turned to the documents of the day. This time, the emails were organized. He recalled being handed the documents individually, not in a folder. About mid-day, Mr. Berger came across another version of the MAAR. In October, Mr. Berger saw a version of the MAAR and now had doubts that what he removed in September was the final report. At this point, he wanted to track the evolution of the MAAR. He slid the document under his portfolio.

███ told Mr. Berger there was a missing document, one that ███ could not find. Mr. Berger b6,
said at this point "the bomb should have burst in the air, but obviously it did not." However, Mr. b7c
Berger did apprehend the consequences of what ███ said. Mr. Berger disassembled first, then he
asked ███ if the document could have been misfiled. ███████ said "No." Mr. Berger asked if they
had not produced this document already. ███████ said it was a different version.

███████ gave him another copy of the document. Mr. Berger slid this document under his portfolio b6,
also. ███████ did not ask for it back. If ███ had asked for it back, it would have "triggered" a b7c
decision for him to give the documents back.

In total, he removed four documents, all versions of the MAAR. Mr. Berger does not recall if he placed all the documents on his person at once or at different times. He did not put the documents on his person until he was alone. He removed the notes, about fifteen pages, towards the end of the day.

Mr. Berger had a long day and wanted to go home around 6 p.m. ██████ wanted him to finish the b2
review and said they only had about an hours worth of work left. He understood ███ was getting b6,b
pressure from the White House to provide a response so he agreed. ███████ suggested he take a
walk and come back and finish up. Mr. Berger left the building with all the documents he put in his
pockets. He was aware of the risk he was taking, but he also knew ████████████
█████████

Mr. Berger exited the Archives on to Pennsylvania Avenue, the north entrance. It was dark. He did b6
not want to run the risk of bringing the documents back in the building risking the possibility ██████ b
might notice something unusual. He headed towards a construction area on Ninth Street. Mr. Berger
looked up and down the street, up into the windows of the Archives and the DOJ, and did not see
anyone. He removed the documents from his pockets, folded the notes in a "V" shape and inserted
the documents in the center. He walked inside the construction fence and slid the documents under
a trailer.

Mr. Berger came back into the building without fearing the documents might slip out of his pockets or b2
that ███████ and ███ staff would notice that his pockets were bulging. ██████████ b6,!

If Mr. Berger had been aware ██████████ staff was tracking the documents he was provided, he b6
would not have removed them. He also said that if staff had escorted him out of the building for his b7
walk, he would have felt less confident that no one was in the area and someone might be watching b2
his actions.

Case Number: ██████ b2	Case Title: Samuel R. Berger ██████ b2

NARA - OIG Form OI 203 (Rev 04/2005)

Office of Inspector General
National Archives and Records Administration

Edited by W. Frederick Zimmerman, NIMBLE BOOKS LLC

NIMBLE BOOKS LLC

ISBN: 0-9788138-5-5

Library of Congress Pre-assigned Control Number (PCN): N/A

This document last saved **2007-03-06.**

Table of Contents

Readers and reviewers, here's what to expect

This book gathers recent, credible, public information about former Clinton National Security Adviser Sandy Berger's appalling theft of classified materials from the National Archives.

If you or I had done what he did, we would be in jail.

Read this book if ...

- You respect the National Archives.
- You believe government officials should fulfill their legal obligations to protect classified information.
- You respect the rule of law.

Don't bother if ...

- You aren't interested in hearing anything negative about a Democrat.

About the author

W. Frederick Zimmerman is the publisher of Nimble Books LLC.

About Nimble Books

Our trusty Merriam-Webster Collegiate Dictionary defines "nimble" as follows:

> 1: quick and light in motion: AGILE *nimble fingers*

> 2 a: marked by quick, alert, clever conception, comprehension, or resourcefulness *a nimble mind* b: RESPONSIVE, SENSITIVE *a nimble listener*

And traces the etymology to the 14th Century:

> Middle English nimel, from Old English numol holding much, from niman to take; akin to Old High German neman to take, Greek nemein to distribute, manage, nomos pasture, nomos usage, custom, law

The etymology is reminiscent of the old Biblical adage, "to whom much is given, much is expected" (Luke 12:48). Nimble Books seeks to honor that Christian principle by combining the spirit of *nimbleness* with the Biblical concept of *abundance:* we deliver what you need to know about a subject in a quick, resourceful, and sensitive manner.

Acknowledgements

Cheryl, Kelsey, and Parker, as always.

NIMBLE BOOKS LLC

.

Bloggers

RealClearPolitics.com: *Sandy Berger: What Did He Take and Why Did He Take It?*, By Ronald A. Cass

Some things cry out for explanation. Like finding $90,000 in marked bills in a Congressman's freezer. Or finding out that a blue-chip lawyer who held one of the most important jobs in the nation was willing to risk his career, his livelihood, and his liberty to steal, hide, and destroy classified documents.

We all have a pretty good idea what the money was doing in Representative William Jefferson's freezer. But the questions about President William Jefferson Clinton's National Security Adviser, Sandy Berger, just keep piling up.

It's time we got some answers.

****

According to reports from the Inspector General of the National Archives and the staff of the House of Representatives' Government Operations Committee, Mr. Berger, while acting as former President Clinton's designated representative to the commission investigating the attacks of September 11, 2001, illegally took confidential documents from the Archives on more than one occasion. He folded documents in his clothes, snuck them out of the Archives building, and stashed them under a construction trailer nearby until he could return, retrieve them, and later cut them up. After he was caught, he lied to the investigators and tried to shift blame to Archive employees.

Contrary to his initial denials and later excuses, Berger clearly intended from the outset to remove sensitive material from the Archives. He used the pretext of making and receiving private phone calls to get time alone with confidential material, although rules governing access dictated that someone from the Archives staff must be present. He took bathroom breaks every half-hour to provide further opportunity to remove and conceal documents.

Before this information was released, the Justice Department, accepting his explanation of innocent and accidental removal of the documents, allowed Berger to enter a plea to the misdemeanor charge of unauthorized removal and retention of classified material - no prison time, no loss of his bar license. The series of actions that the Archives and House investigations detail, however, are entirely at odds with protestations of innocence. Nothing about his actions was accidental. Nothing was casual. And nothing was normal.

What could have been important enough for Berger to take the risks he did? What could have been important enough for a lawyer of his distinction to risk disgrace, disbarment, and prison?

To paraphrase the questions asked of Richard Nixon by members of his own Party, what did he take and why did he take it?

****

The report released by Rep. Tom Davis last week makes plain that right now we cannot answer those questions. We cannot say what information in fact was lost through Mr. Berger's actions.

At President Clinton's request, he reviewed highly confidential material during four visits to the Archives over four months. Only Mr. Berger knows what transpired on his first two visits, when he reviewed collections of confidential memos, e-mails, and handwritten notes, including materials taken from counter-terrorism adviser Richard Clarke's office - all of which were not catalogued at the individual item level.

On Mr. Berger's third visit Archives employees became suspicious that he might be removing classified material. Rather than directly confront a former Cabinet-level official, Archives officials simply took steps to identify further theft on succeeding visits. That is how Mr. Berger's thefts on his fourth and last visit were documented.

We don't know what Mr. Berger might have removed from the uncatalogued materials reviewed in his earlier visits, but we know his last visit focused on a memorandum called the Millennium Alert After Action Report (MAAAR). Copies of this report were made available to the 9/11 Commission, but the information in those copies undoubtedly is not what interested Berger most. Berger took five copies of the report and later destroyed three of them.

What was on the copies he destroyed? Handwritten notes from Berger, the President, or some other official? Observations that would be embarrassing to them, evidence they missed an important threat or considered or recommended actions - or decisions not to act - they wouldn't want to defend in public? Evidence, perhaps, that would have supported the Bush Administration? We don't know, and no one who does is saying, but the evidence must have been terribly damning for Berger to take the risks he did.

****

There are good reasons to protect sensitive communications within the government. Some discussions should be private if presidents are to have the best advice and the nation is to have the best decisions on sensitive matters. The President and top officials should be able to explore options and discuss threats - among themselves and with their key staff members - without fear that a remark taken out of context or poorly phrased will come back to haunt them.

Laws that endeavor to strike the balance between salutary confidentiality and beneficial public disclosure at times tilt too far to disclosure. In public debate, advantages of disclosure are often easier to explain than advantages of secrecy. That, in part, follows from the nature of secrets - if you don't reveal them, you can't explain fully why they should have stayed secret.

The Berger episode, however, strictly involves materials that are *supposed* to be turned over under the law, materials specifically covered by a presidential directive that authorized sharing the information with those investigating 9/11 intelligence-gathering and evaluation. Mr. Berger's willingness to risk everything to suppress the information goes well beyond ordinary concerns against excessive disclosure.

Bill Clinton obviously has great sensitivity to his place in history and to accusations that he did too little to respond to al-Qaeda, that he is to some degree responsible for failing to prevent 9/11's tragedy. That is why he and his lieutenants made reckless and baseless accusations against the current Bush administration, attempting to portray them as having dropped the baton handed off by ever-vigilant Clintonistas (who, according to John Ashcroft's testimony, withheld the MAAAR and its warnings about al-Qaeda's operations in the US from the Bush transition team).

But maybe there is more to the story. Maybe there is something far worse than we can imagine that is worth having his chief security aide risk his reputation, his career, and his liberty to cover up.

****

Mr. Berger, the Clintons, and their allies do not want questions about this story asked or answered. Mr. Berger's lawyer, Lanny Breuer, along with former Clinton officials, assured us that all of the material destroyed by Berger existed in other form and was made available to the 9/11 investigations, that nothing relevant to the Clinton Administration's response to al-Qaeda was withheld.

Of course, we also were assured that Monica had only imagined a relationship with Bill and that rumors to the contrary were, in Hillary's famous phrase, the work of a "vast right-wing conspiracy."

Politicians never like to admit mistakes. They see legitimate inquiries as politically inspired, which they often are. Changing the subject or shifting blame to others aren't tactics peculiar to the Clintons.

The Clintons, however, take the game of deny-deceive-and-distract to a new level. Their relentless personal attacks on Ken Starr were designed to undermine the credibility of information about Bill Clinton's perjury, to deflect attention from his own failings. Clinton's excessive reaction - complete with hyperbole, finger-wagging, and scolding - to a simple question from Fox News' Chris Wallace about his response to al-Qaeda is in the same vein. Something here touches a nerve.

That nerve is exposed in the Sandy Berger saga. This story at bottom is about the security of our nation, about what was - or was not - done to protect us from the most shocking and deadly attack on American citizens by foreign agents in our nation's history. This story is critical not only to understanding our past but also to securing our future. It can help us understand what it is reasonable to expect can be done to keep us and our loved ones safe from harm. It is, in short, as important a story as there is.

****

It is a story the news media should be desperate to explore, not desperate to avoid.

They should want to know the full story, no matter what the implications are for the legacy of a president much loved by an overwhelmingly liberal media or what the risks are for a former First Lady whose future is tied to her husband's past. Those risks loom especially large before a field of potential Republican presidential candidates with strong reputations in security matters - like Rudy Giuliani, for example, whose courageous performance on 9/11 still resonates.

Those who wrap themselves so frequently in the mantra of the people's right to know should want to know the truth - all the time. Sadly, today's would-be Woodwards and Bernsteins look more like ostriches than hawks, showing no curiosity about what Sandy Berger was hiding. Had that been the attitude when Watergate first appeared as a minor news story, Richard Nixon would have served out his full second term. The rest, as they say, is history.

Mr. Cass, Chairman of the Center for the Rule of Law and Dean Emeritus of Boston University School of Law, served Presidents Ronald Reagan and George H.W. Bush as Commissioner and Vice-Chairman of the US International Trade Commission.

Guntoting Liberal: <u>*Security clearances - "liberally" issued to, "conservatively" revoked from the "Elites"; "conservatively" issued to, and "liberally" revoked from the "pleebs".*</u>

WOW… just because Sandy Berger has a "D" behind his name shouldn't leave him out of ANY tirade against violations of the Peoples' Trust in him for this nation's security. Any and ALL people who intentionally violate this nation's security for political, personal, and/or financial gain like Sandy Berger has done, and like Scooter Libby has done, and perhaps even our Vice President has done, MUST be PUNISHED.

I take this issue quite personally. Recently, as I've watched Plamegate, Sandy Berger, and President Bush's political game (a.k.a., the game of "Classify/Declassify for political gain") with classified info unravel, I've watched a family member; a regular, hard working guy with a government issued "secret" clearance have it suddenly suspended because a random, periodic check revealed a few items that were being misreported fraudulently on his credit report by one of "The Big Three" credit reporting agencies. Those items were not accurate; he is still trying to straighten it out. Perhaps, he is only guilty of "Blogging Successfully from the Left" (identity and URL witheld)?

Meanwhile, he has almost lost his job, and is only allowed to perform certain portions of it, UNDER supervision. He is considered a "national threat" until those creditors resubmit — PROPERLY — the CRA information on his file. He is not only a so-called "security risk", he is also a BURDEN upon his employer and coworkers as a result of this SNAFU.

Yet, Sandy Berger is rumored to have been assured that he should have his clearance reinstated sometime this year, and I doubt that Scooter Libbys' has even been revoked yet. My friend put his homelife on hold in support of Operation Iraqi Freedom; Scooter Libby outed a CIA agent's identity. My friend ingested and breathed the fine sands of the Middle East, Sandy Berger stuffed his pockets full of classified documents. My friend SERVED, these people PREYED; my friend's good name STILL remains in limbo; most of the above remain free and unhindered in any way for their ACTUAL transgressions against the trust of the American People.

Where's the justice? Why play "politics" with something as serious as this? What we NEED to do is take our country back and deliver her into the laps of the Citizens again, where she belongs. To HELL with "politics". There are some things you just do not play "games" with, and national security is one of them… and if YOU are playing "games" with our national security in order to influence elections… what makes you any different from the rest of the above-mentioned ominous cast of characters?

MEMORANDUM OF INTERVIEW
OR ACTIVITY

Type of Activity:	Date and Time:
☒ Personal Interview ☐ Telephone Interview ☐ Records Review ☐ Other	July 8, 2005 9:30 a.m.

Activity or Interview of:	Conducted by:
Samuel R. Berger	▮▮▮▮▮▮▮ b6, b7C
	Location of Interview/Activity: Washington, DC

Subject Matter/Remarks

On July 8, 2005, ▮▮▮▮▮▮▮▮▮▮▮▮▮▮▮▮▮▮▮▮▮▮▮▮▮▮▮▮   b6, b7C
▮▮▮▮▮▮▮▮▮▮▮▮ interviewed Samuel "Sandy" R. Berger, former National Security Advisor (NSA) to President William J. Clinton, at the Bond Building, 1400 New York Avenue, Washington, DC. Mr. Berger participated as part of his plea agreement.

Also present were ▮▮▮ b6
▮▮   b7C
▮▮

Mr. Berger described his personality as intense and a uni-tasker. He did not believe anyone would describe him as arrogant. He did not feel he was overbearing and did not seek to intimidate anyone while at the Archives. Mr. Berger provided the following information:

Mr. Berger visited the Archives, Washington, DC, to review documents requested from the Clinton Presidential materials. Mr. Berger did not have a vivid recollection of visiting the Archives on May 30, 2002, to review documents in preparation for his testimony before the Graham-Goss / Joint Intelligence Committee. Mr. Berger did recall his visits to the Archives to review documents to determine if Executive Privilege needed to be exerted prior to documents being provided to the National Commission on Terrorist Attacks Upon the United States (hereafter, the 9/11 Commission).

On every visit to the Archives, Mr. Berger came in the Pennsylvania Avenue entrance of the Archives, proceeded through the magnetometer, and signed a log book at the security desk. Someone from   b6,
security called ▮▮▮▮▮▮▮▮▮▮▮▮▮▮▮▮▮▮▮▮▮▮▮▮▮▮▮▮▮▮, office and someone from b7C
▮▮▮▮▮▮▮ office would escort Mr. Berger to ▮▮▮▮▮▮▮ office. Mr. Berger always left late in the

Case Number: ▮▮▮ b2	Case Title: Samuel R. Berger▮▮▮ b2

NARA - OIG Form OI 203 (Rev 04/2005)

MEMORANDUM OF INTERVIEW OR ACTIVITY (continuation sheet)   2

evening, around 7 p.m. There were no guards in the lobby at that time. Therefore, no one ever checked his belongings on his way out.

██████ was very professional and courteous. However, ██ was not warm and "fuzzy" with Mr. b6
Berger. ████████ told Mr. Berger he could take notes while he was at the Archives but ██ made it b7
clear he could not remove them. He did not understand the documents could have been sent to the
National Security Council (NSC) for review and classification. [Mr. Berger did ask that his notes from
his May 2002 review be sent to the NSC for review. The NSC returned his notes as classified.] He
did understand the notes would remain at the Archives for him to use on subsequent visits.

All document reviews by Mr. Berger were conducted in ████████ office. Mr. Berger sat at a small b6
table in ██ office. ████████ did not brief Mr. Berger on security procedures. ██ must have b7C
assumed a briefing was not required due to his previous positions as the NSA. ████ did not
advise Mr. Berger on what he could and could not bring into the Archives. ████ did not provide
Mr. Berger paper. On every visit, Mr. Berger brought his leather portfolio with a note pad inside. It
was his practice to wear a suit but he did not recall if he wore a coat to the Archives.

Mr. Berger did not believe he received preferential treatment until after his visits when he learned ██ b7
████ office was not an appropriate facility to view classified material. Mr. Berger believed he was b6,
afforded the opportunity to review documents in a more comfortable environment after someone
described the ██████████████████████████████ accommodations to him. At the b7
time of his review, Mr. Berger did not know nor did he consider the nature of ████ office and
whether ████████. He believed he was in a suitable location to review the documents. Mr.
Berger did not consider asking that the documents be sent to another location for review as he was
not aware of another convenient location to conduct the review.

Mr. Berger stated ██████████████████████████████████ of the protocol b1
in reviewing these records ████ his notes had to remain at the Archives and the Archives would b7
send them to the NSC for classification.

Mr. Berger made a general statement that he went to the restroom on an average of every thirty b6,
minutes to one hour to use the facilities and stretch his legs. This was the only room he went to b7C
besides ████████ office.

Mr. Berger explained that after 9/11, the Clinton Administration was inundated with calls on their
response to this terrorist attack. It was obvious he was going to have to testify on their actions. Mr.
Berger put in over 100 hours of his time, unpaid, in order to be responsive. Everyone else stepped
back from the questions but Mr. Berger felt responsible.

Mr. Berger reviewed the documents at the Archives not only for privilege but also to refresh his b5,
recollection for his testimony and assisting in preparing others ████████████████ b
████████████ for their testimony. ████
████ only had tangential contact with the records. Mr. Berger had unique knowledge of the records
and the appropriate clearances.

Case Number: ████ b2 | Case Title: Samuel R. Berger████ b2

NARA - OIG Form OI 203 (Rev 04/2005)

Office of Inspector General
National Archives and Records Administration

MEMORANDUM OF INTERVIEW OR ACTIVITY (continuation sheet)   3

In May or June 2003, ████████ called Mr. Berger to say █ received a request from the 9/11   b6,
Commission. ████████ acted as the liaison between the Clinton Administration and the Archives.
████████ asked Mr. Berger to go to the Archives to review records in response to the Executive   b7c
Office of the President's (EOP) requests.

On **July 18, 2003**, Mr. Berger reviewed material in response to EOP 2. The boxes of materials were b6
on a cart in ████████ office between Mr. Berger's seat and the coffee table, or off to his side. ██
██ handed Mr. Berger "bunches" of folders. Once he completed the review, ██ would hand him b7c
another bunch. If ██ was not sitting with Mr. Berger, ████████ was working at ██ desk, usually on
the computer at an angle to him where he could see ██ over his right shoulder.

The documents were not organized chronologically. Mr. Berger would read the documents, trying to b6
save all his questions instead of interrupting ████████ work. He was trying to be sensitive to ██
work responsibilities. ████████ and Mr. Berger would read over the documents on which he had b7c
questions. ████████ ruled on responsiveness to the 9/11 Commission.

There were more questions to be answered in July 2003, as this was the first EOP request he was b6,
involved with. Some of the questions included what constitutes a document, does the 9/11
Commission want duplicate copies of the same information, do they want copies of the same b7c
document that contained additional notes, etc. There were two or three calls to ████████ on these
issues during Mr. Berger's review.

Mr. Berger started his own company, Stonebridge, in 2001. ████████████████, had ██ b6
████ phone number from setting up appointments for Mr. Berger's visits. He told his secretary not
to call him at the Archives unless there was a time sensitive issue. His secretary probably called him b7
at ████████ number about a half dozen times on this visit. Mr. Berger told ████████ he was happy
to go outside ██ office to take the calls. ████████ asked Mr. Berger if he needed privacy to which
he said "yes." ████████ said instead that ██ would go outside ██ office while he was on the
phone, which ██ did. Once this pattern was established, he thought the offer for ██ to leave ██
office was "standing." ████████████████████████████████. Mr. Berger
had no intent to order ██ out of ██ office. While Mr. Berger was on the phone, he was left alone in
████████ office. He used the phone closest to the couch. It was a hard line and he wanted that
privacy with his clients. Mr. Berger did not use his cell phone and never told ████ ████ it was not
working.

Mr. Berger could not recall specifically if ████████ left ██ office when ██ made phone calls. The b6
only other time ████████ left ██ office during his reviews was maybe to step out to get more boxes
or consult with ██ staff. He did not recall if any of ████████ staff stepped in the office with him b7c
when ██ stepped for these moments. Mr. Berger did not take any breaks to leave the building
during this visit.

██ b6
██. At some point, Mr. Berger took b7
notes. He realized he was not going to be able to reconstruct in detail all the documents he had
reviewed, so he needed to take his notes with him, about ten to twenty pages.

Case Number: b2	Case Title: Samuel R. Berger ████ b2

Office of Inspector General
National Archives and Records Administration

MEMORANDUM Or INTERVIEW OR ACTIVITY (continuation sheet)   4

At the end of the day, Mr. Berger tri-folded his notes and put them in his suit pocket. He took the   b6,
opportunity to do this when ▮▮▮▮▮ was out of ▮▮ office due to him being on a private phone call.   b7
Mr. Berger said he did not recall being hesitant to remove his suit jacket during this visit. However, at
some point, him not removing his jacket could have been related to the fact he placed the notes in his
jacket. Mr. Berger knew he had to leave some notes behind so it would not be obvious he removed
notes. He had been making notes and if he did not leave any behind it would have been noticeable.
[Mr. Berger was surprised to learn he left only two pages of notes at the Archives.]

The notes he removed were torn from the top of the note pad. Mr. Berger did not have time to sort
through and determine which pages he wanted to take and which to leave. He said this was the
scenario on all three occasions when he removed notes from the Archives. He was aware he would
not have a complete set but some notes were better than none.

Mr. Berger did not recall asking ▮▮▮▮▮▮ to have the documents arranged chronologically on his   b6,b7C
next visit. However, he might have mentioned they were not arranged chronologically.

The Millennium Alert After Action Review (MAAR) should have been with the documents Mr. Berger
was reviewing on this visit, but he does not recall seeing it. The Principals meeting was in June 2000
and invariably before these meetings a memo reflecting what they were going to talk about would   b6,
have been circulated. The Principals consisted of the ▮▮▮▮▮▮▮▮▮▮▮▮▮▮▮▮▮▮▮▮▮▮▮▮▮▮▮   b7C
▮▮▮▮▮▮▮▮▮▮▮▮▮▮▮▮▮▮▮▮▮▮▮▮▮▮▮▮▮▮▮▮▮▮▮▮▮▮▮, and others.

Mr. Berger did not remove any documents on this visit.

▮▮▮▮▮▮▮▮▮ came to the Archives in July 2003, to review documents in response to EOP 2. Mr.   b6,
Berger did not ask ▮▮▮▮▮▮▮ to look for the MAAR or any other specific documents.   b7C

On **September 2, 2003**, Mr. Berger came to the Archives to review documents in response to EOP 3.   b6,
Again, the boxes of materials were on a cart in ▮▮▮▮▮▮ office between Mr. Berger's seat and the
coffee table, or off to his side. ▮▮▮▮▮▮ was working with Mr. Berger in the review of the   b7C
documents. ▮▮▮▮▮ spent about the same amount of time with Mr. Berger as ▮▮ had on his visit
in July 2003. Mr. Berger could not estimate a percentage on the amount of time. His recollection
was that the documents were Xerox copies.

Again, ▮▮▮▮▮▮ always stepped out of ▮ office when Mr. Berger made or received phone calls.   b6,
▮▮ may have also stepped out to consult with ▮ staff, for a minute, but he has no recollection of   b7C
whether ▮ staff would step in when ▮ was out.

Mr. Berger was not told anything about the process of the documents after his review and their
presentation to the 9/11 Commission. It never occurred to Mr. Berger that by removing the MAAR
from the Archives, it would not be provided to the 9/11 Commission. It was his assumption the box of
documents he was reviewing at the Archives, or a copy of them, was going from the Archives to the

Case Number: ▮▮▮▮ b2	Case Title: Samuel R. Berger ▮▮▮▮ b2

MEMORANDUM OF INTERVIEW OR ACTIVITY (continuation sheet)   5

White House. He did not assume that his removal of documents kept them from going forward to the 9/11 Commission. Mr. Berger knew he was not reviewing originals.

In late November and early December 1999, there were five to fifteen [terrorist] attacks. During this time, the Principals met every day for about an hour. They were operating more like a working group to get though the millennium. During this time, Ahmed Ressam was caught in Washington State with explosives to be used at the Los Angeles International Airport.

After the millennium, Mr. Berger asked ▮▮▮▮▮▮▮▮▮▮▮▮▮▮▮▮▮▮▮▮▮▮▮▮▮, to prepare the MAAR to determine where they were exposed and the vulnerabilities. There were fights over the jurisdiction of the funding. In March 2001, the Principals approved the recommendations and they were funded. After 9/11, the MAAR was widely discussed in the press. Mr. Berger commented the MAAR was not the most sensitive document he reviewed at the Archives.

Mr. Berger believed the MAAR was widely distributed among the FBI, the CIA, and the Department of State, for a total of about fifteen people. The MAAR was circulated three to four times to four or five people at each agency. All these agencies were subject to the EOP requests. ▮▮▮▮▮▮ was going to testify concerning the MAAR.

Mr. Berger read through the MAAR and took notes. There were twenty-nine topics for recommendations under four categories. He thought the 9/11 Commission would want to know what the Clinton Administration did to "fill in the holes." He was trying to move quickly through the document review. ▮▮▮▮▮▮ had told him he still had three more days' worth of documents to review. Mr. Berger now says it was a foolish decision to take the MAAR and the notes out of the Archives.

Mr. Berger believed this MAAR to be the final report. However, this would have been more likely if this version had a cover page/sheet. Mr. Berger did not return the MAAR to the pile that was returned to ▮▮▮▮. He did not have a recollection of putting other documents in this folder but he did have the intent to take the document. [There were two documents in what had been an empty folder after he removed the MAAR. ▮▮▮ archivists did not move any documents into this folder.] He did not put any intentional markings on the documents. Mr. Berger did not recall receiving this folder separately from other folders. He did not recall seeing any other versions of the MAAR on this visit.

During this visit, Mr. Berger received more calls as there were two op-ed articles out. One article stated Sudan offered Osama Bin Laden to the United States in 1996 but the Clinton Administration did not take the offer. Mr. Berger referred to this as an urban legend. The other article was by former Secretary of Defense Casper Weinberger who said the Clinton Administration was responsible for the attacks on September 11, 2001. These articles initiated a "flurry" of activities.

Mr. Berger took the first opportunity when ▮▮▮▮▮ was out of ▮▮ office to remove the document. He most likely put it in his jacket pocket, after folding it, but he does not have a precise recollection of where he put the document. It is perceivable he put it in his pants pocket. It was also possible he placed it in his portfolio and took it out. The document was twelve to thirteen pages. The notes were folded and put in his pocket. He would have put the notes on his person at the end of the day.

Case Number: ▮▮▮▮ ϧ7	Case Title: Samuel R. Berger▮▮ ϧ7

NARA - OIG Form OI 203 (Rev 04/2005)

Mr. Berger did not believe [REDACTED] personnel were suspicious that he was removing documents. They did not give him any indications of this.

Mr. Berger denied removing any documents in his socks. [He asked us to describe what the potential witness saw, which we did.] He stated his shoes frequently come untied [To which [REDACTED] said he was a witness.] and his socks frequently fall down. [At that point, Mr. Berger lifted his pant leg to reveal a sock falling down his ankle and pale skin.] Besides, it would have fallen out of his sock. He said this story was absurd and embarrassing.

After leaving the Archives for the day, Mr. Berger went back to his office and put the document in an envelope on his desk.

On September 2, 2003, Mr. Berger called someone who was helping him review materials. He told them they should be prepared to answer the 9/11 Commission's questions concerning the MAAR.

It was asked that [REDACTED]; former Clinton staffer, be cleared to review these documents. Mr. Berger had not worked on a document search in thirty years. If he was working at the NSC, this is certainly something someone on his staff would have done for him. [REDACTED] was able to [REDACTED] [REDACTED] cleared for [REDACTED] material but the [REDACTED] clearance.

On **October 2, 2003**, Mr. Berger was reviewing documents at the Archives. The documents were in accordion files. [REDACTED] had the documents in a box, on the floor, by [REDACTED] desk. The time [REDACTED] spent with him in reviewing the documents did not change. He did not recall NARA staff being more or less restrictive with the documents than on other visits.

[REDACTED] first provided Mr. Berger the documents marked for review by [REDACTED]. A version of the MAAR was with these documents, marked [REDACTED]. Mr. Berger did not know why it was classified differently than the version he removed in September which was [REDACTED]. It was obvious to him this was a different version of the MAAR. Mr. Berger wanted to know how it was edited to now be classified as [REDACTED]. He needed to compare the two versions of the MAAR. [REDACTED] had mentioned the MAAR went through several iterations but the changes were over money not substantive. Mr. Berger placed this version under his portfolio while [REDACTED] assistant was in the office. He then returned the folder to [REDACTED] assistant. Mr. Berger has no recollection of post-it notes on this document or moving them to another document. The assistant was standing in the area by [REDACTED] desk where the files were.

Next, [REDACTED] provided him all but two documents the White House had sent back from the documents he reviewed for EOP 2. [The White House sent those two documents on to the 9/11 Commission.]

[REDACTED]

Case Number: [REDACTED] b2	Case Title: Samuel R. Berger [REDACTED] b2

MEMORANDUM O. INTERVIEW OR ACTIVITY (cu.ituation sheet)   7

Then they turned to the documents of the day. This time, the emails were organized. He recalled being handed the documents individually, not in a folder. About mid-day, Mr. Berger came across another version of the MAAR. In October, Mr. Berger saw a version of the MAAR and now had doubts that what he removed in September was the final report. At this point, he wanted to track the evolution of the MAAR. He slid the document under his portfolio.

███████ told Mr. Berger there was a missing document, one that ███ could not find. Mr. Berger   b6₁
said at this point "the bomb should have burst in the air, but obviously it did not." However, Mr.   b7C
Berger did apprehend the consequences of what ███ said. Mr. Berger disassembled first, then he
asked ███ if the document could have been misfiled. ███████ said "No." Mr. Berger asked if they
had not produced this document already. ████████ said it was a different version.

███████ gave him another copy of the document. Mr. Berger slid this document under his portfolio   b6₁
also. ████████ did not ask for it back. If ███ had asked for it back, it would have "triggered" a   b7C
decision for him to give the documents back.

In total, he removed four documents, all versions of the MAAR. Mr. Berger does not recall if he placed all the documents on his person at once or at different times. He did not put the documents on his person until he was alone. He removed the notes, about fifteen pages, towards the end of the day.

Mr. Berger had a long day and wanted to go home around 6 p.m. ████████ wanted him to finish the   b2
review and said they only had about an hours worth of work left. He understood ███ was getting   b6,b
pressure from the White House to provide a response so he agreed. ████████ suggested he take a
walk and come back and finish up. Mr. Berger left the building with all the documents he put in his
pockets. He was aware of the risk he was taking, but he also knew ████████████████
██████.

Mr. Berger exited the Archives on to Pennsylvania Avenue, the north entrance. It was dark. He did   b6
not want to run the risk of bringing the documents back in the building risking the possibility ██████   b-
might notice something unusual. He headed towards a construction area on Ninth Street. Mr. Berger
looked up and down the street, up into the windows of the Archives and the DOJ, and did not see
anyone. He removed the documents from his pockets, folded the notes in a "V" shape and inserted
the documents in the center. He walked inside the construction fence and slid the documents under
a trailer.

Mr. Berger came back into the building without fearing the documents might slip out of his pockets or   b2
that █████████ and ███ staff would notice that his pockets were bulging. ████████████████
██████   b6,₁

If Mr. Berger had been aware ████████ staff was tracking the documents he was provided, he   b6
would not have removed them. He also said that if staff had escorted him out of the building for his   b2
walk, he would have felt less confident that no one was in the area and someone might be watching
his actions.

Case Number: ███████ b2	Case Title: Samuel R. Berger ████ b2

NARA - OIG Form OI 203 (Rev 04/2005)

MEMORANDUM O₁ INTERVIEW OR ACTIVITY (continuation sheet)   8

Mr. Berger does not recall reviewing his notes or ▮▮▮▮▮▮▮▮ notes on this visit. b6,b7C

It is possible that ▮▮▮▮▮▮▮▮▮▮▮▮▮▮▮▮▮▮▮▮▮▮▮▮, stopped by to introduce ▮▮▮▮ but Mr. Berger did not have a vivid memory of this.   b6,b7C

Mr. Berger was trying to balance his review carefully but was also trying to be expeditious. He skipped meals and drank diet cokes. He did go to the restroom, possibly with documents in his pockets, but did not discard documents there or rearrange them on his person.

On this visit, ▮▮   b6,b7C
▮▮▮▮▮▮▮▮▮▮▮▮▮▮▮▮▮▮▮▮▮▮▮▮▮▮▮▮▮

▮▮▮▮▮ did not tell Mr. Berger that ▮▮ had numbered the documents or that ▮▮ had a way of b6,
tracking these records. Mr. Berger said he would have "picked-up" on that comment. He said "I may b7C
be stupid, but I am not self destructive." As he left for the day between 7 and 7:30 p.m., ▮▮▮▮▮▮
asked Mr. Berger ▮▮▮▮▮▮▮▮▮▮▮▮▮▮▮▮▮▮▮▮▮▮▮▮▮▮▮▮▮ He totally missed
that signal later realizing it was ▮▮ subtle way to ask him if he removed documents. Mr. Berger
believed no one knew he removed documents.

Mr. Berger left the building, retrieved the documents and notes from the construction area, and returned to his office.

On **October 4, 2003**, late in the afternoon, ▮▮▮▮▮▮▮ called Mr. Berger to tell him ▮▮▮▮▮ called   b6,
from the Archives. Mr. Berger was aware ▮▮▮▮▮ was the ▮▮▮▮▮▮▮▮▮▮▮▮▮▮▮▮▮▮▮▮▮▮▮ b7C
▮▮▮▮▮ said documents were missing after Mr. Berger's visit on October 2, 2003. Mr. Berger panicked
because he realized he was caught. Mr. Berger lied to ▮▮▮▮▮ telling ▮▮ he did not take the
documents.

Mr. Berger remembers next calling ▮▮▮▮▮▮▮ at ▮▮ office. He knew it was not a good sign ▮▮ was   b6
there on a Saturday. ▮▮ described the documents stating there were four copies of three   b7C
documents missing. Mr. Berger asked ▮▮ if the four documents they were missing were copies of
the MAAR. He told ▮▮▮▮▮▮ he would see if he accidentally took them. Mr. Berger was agitated
because he realized he was caught.

▮▮▮▮▮ called Mr. Berger and said "I hope you can find them because if not, we have to refer this to   b3
the NSC's ▮▮▮▮▮▮▮▮." ▮▮▮▮▮ did not say what would be done if Mr. Berger returned the   b6,b7C
documents. When asked again, Mr. Berger became unsure whether ▮▮▮▮▮▮ said
this to him. However, he was sure the source of the statement was ▮▮▮▮▮▮ asked Mr.
Berger to go to his office to see if he could find the documents.

Mr. Berger drove to his office late that afternoon. On the night of October 2, 2003, he had destroyed, b6,
cut into small pieces, three of the four documents. These were put in the trash. By Saturday, the
trash had been picked-up. He tried to find the trash collector but had no luck. Neither ▮▮▮▮▮ nor   b7C
▮▮▮▮▮ offered to help him look through the trash.

Case Number: ▮▮▮▮ b2	Case Title: Samuel R. Berger ▮▮▮▮ b2

MEMORANDUM O, INTERVIEW OR ACTIVITY (continuation sheet)   9

About 7 p.m., Mr. Berger called ███████ and said "I think I solved the mystery." ███ said █   bb
was going into ████ and would call as soon as it was over. About 11:30 p.m., Mr. ███ called Mr.
Berger. Mr. Berger told ██, "I found two documents but not the other two." ████████ told him to get   b7
the documents from his office and lock them in the safe in his home. ████████ was glad he found
two but three were still missing.

Mr. Berger did not recall ███████████, unless ██ picked-up the documents.   bb,b7C

On **October 5, 2003**, Mr. Berger recalled NARA staff picking up the two documents at his home. He
understands that NARA staff recalled picking up the documents at his office. Mr. Berger was willing
to accept that NARA staff came to his office.

There were additional conference calls. ███████ was surprised when Mr. Berger returned the   bb,b7C
documents he removed in September. He knew he was caught, so he purported he must have
removed the documents accidentally or inadvertently by sweeping them up with his documents.
Later, Mr. Berger made a decision, on his own, to tell the truth. He said "I realized I was giving a
benign explanation for what was not benign." Mr. Berger wanted to return everything he had taken.
He realized he was returning documents he removed in September. He did not realize he returned
more than they knew he removed. Mr. Berger was aware of the consequences but he knew returning
the documents was the right thing to do.

Mr. Berger called ███████████ told ███ what happened, and asked what he should do. ████████   bb,
told Mr. Berger to get a lawyer. Mr. Berger and ███████████ did not discuss this issue any further as   b7C
they were ███████████ and knew it was better not to talk about this.

Mr. Berger specifically recalled returning his notes to NARA staff at his home. He had flown in from
New York, spent about an hour at his home, then flew back to New York to continue his travel. NARA
staff never mentioned his notes. Mr. Berger believed if he had not returned them, they would never
have known he removed his notes.

Mr. Berger does not know ████████████████████████████████, nor did he have any   bb,
contact with ███. Mr. Berger had not met ███████████ prior to these visits to the Archives. Additionally,   b7
he did not contact the NSC on this matter.

There were not any handwritten notes on the documents Mr. Berger removed from the Archives. Mr.
Berger did not believe there was unique information in the three documents he destroyed. Mr. Berger
never made any copies of these documents.

Mr. Berger said as a general point, he has dealt with classified information for twelve years. Some
documents are sensitive and some are not super sensitive. This may not have anything to do with
the documents classification. Other documents he reviewed had more sensitive information in them
such as the Presidential Findings. He had seen most of the information in the MAAR disclosed in the
press. He substituted his sense of sensitivity instead of thinking of classification. The MAAR did not
involve sources and methods. It was a policy document.

Case Number: ███████ b2	Case Title: Samuel R. Berger ███████ b2

NARA - OIG Form OI 203 (Rev 04/2005)

MEMORANDUM O. INTERVIEW OR ACTIVITY (cu.tinuation sheet)   10

Some of the notes he removed did have information about the Presidential Findings. This was the authority from the President for actions to be taken.

███████ had no reason to believe he was not acting in an appropriate manner. Mr. Berger said if there was always someone with him, he would not have taken any documents. After learning he was given special treatment by viewing the documents in ████████ office, he suggested no exceptions to the rules should be given to former National Security Advisors or others. The Archives should *b6,b7C* thoroughly check people when they enter and exit the building.

Mr. Berger received enough phone calls which gave him the opportunity to remove the documents. He never sent ████████ out of the room for the sole purpose of removing the documents. *b6, b7C*

The DOJ asked Mr. Berger if he removed any other documents from the Archives that we were not aware of to which Mr. Berger replied no.

Sandy Berger's Theft of Classified Documents: Unanswered Questions

Staff Report
U.S. House of Representatives
110th Congress
Committee on Oversight and Government Reform

Tom Davis, Ranking Member
January 9, 2007

Table of Contents

I. Executive Summary

In May 2002 and in the summer and fall of 2003, President Clinton's former National Security Advisor Sandy Berger visited the National Archives and Records Administration (hereinafter, National Archives or Archives) to review highly classified documents in preparation for being interviewed by a Congressional panel and the 9/11 Commission. In addition to preparing for testimony, Berger was to conduct a Presidential privilege review of documents responsive to official 9/11 Commission requests. The documents were "code word" documents and only a very small number of people had the security clearance to view them – mostly National Security Council officials. It is now known that on these visits Berger unlawfully removed some of the documents he examined. In the Spring of 2005, Berger pleaded guilty to this.

The release of the Archives Inspector General's report and the further inquiry reflected in this report now reveal the extraordinary lengths to which Berger was willing to go to deliberately compromise national security, apparently for his own convenience. The criminal case involved documents that Berger was caught removing and ultimately admitted removing. There is no reason to doubt that those documents were forwarded to the 9/11 Commission for its use. The Justice Department and the Archives apparently accounted for them all and assured the 9/11 Commission that it received them all.

The full extent of Berger's document removal, however, is not known, and never can be known. The Justice Department cannot be sure that Berger did not remove original documents for which there were no copies or inventory. On three of Berger's four visits to the Archives, he had access to such documents.

During Berger's visits to the National Archives, he was provided access to three categories of documents: original NSC numbered documents, printed copies of electronic mail messages and attachments, and uncopied, original Staff Member Office Files (SMOFs). NSC numbered documents are briefing and position papers prepared by the staff of the National Security Council. The SMOFs contain the working papers of White House staff members, including Berger and terrorism advisor Richard Clarke. The contents of the SMOFs are not inventoried by the National Archives at the document level. The SMOFs provided to Berger during his first two visits to the National Archives – including the personal office files of Richard Clarke – contained only original documents.

Consequently, the Department of Justice could not assure the 9/11 Commission that it received all responsive documents to which Berger had access. Additionally, the 9/11 Commission was not informed that Berger had access to original documents that he could have removed without anyone's knowledge. Officials from the National Archives, the Office of Inspector General for the National Archives, and the Department of Justice have acknowledged there is absolutely no way to determine if Berger removed any of these original documents. Because the Staff Member Office Files are not inventoried at the document level, Berger could have removed critical documents and no official would ever be able to know.

While the Staff Member Office Files provide the greatest opportunity for missing documents, the NSC numbered documents also present a serious problem. The NSC numbered documents are only numbered at the document level, not by page. Berger could have removed portions of NSC numbered documents and the National Archives officials would never know. Because Berger was provided with so many original documents, there is no way to ever know if the 9/11 Commission received all required materials.

The facts of this case raise some peculiar and disturbing questions about the conduct, and more importantly, the motivations of the former National Security Advisor. For example, Berger admitted to leaving highly classified documents at a construction site near the main National Archives facility in downtown Washington, D.C. where they could have been easily found. Additionally, one of the archivists with a very high clearance level (and therefore presumably reliable) who worked on the document production for the 9/11 Commission reported that he saw Berger hiding some documents in his socks and under his pants. These acts of concealment show the lengths to which Berger was willing to deliberately go to compromise national security.

More than previously understood, Berger's actions portray a disturbing breach of trust and protocol that compromised the nation's national security. This report examines the specific facts concerning Berger's four visits to the National Archives, the lax procedures in effect at the Archives that allowed these events to unfold, the effects Berger's actions had on the work of the 9/11 Commission, and the actions by the Department of Justice in advising the 9/11 Commission of relevant facts concerning Berger's Archives visits.

II. Findings

- On May 30, 2002, Sandy Berger reviewed original NSC numbered documents and original Staff Member Office Files, including the office files of White House terrorism advisor Richard Clarke. After receiving document requests from the 9/11 Commission in 2003, Archives staff made available the same original document files Berger reviewed in May 2002.

- On July 18, 2003, after reviewing original NSC numbered documents and original Staff Member Office Files, Sandy Berger removed the classified notes he took on that visit.

- On September 2, 2003, after reviewing original NSC numbered documents, copies of Staff Member Office Files, and copies of e-mail documents, Sandy Berger removed classified documents from the

Archives. He admitted to removing a classified version of the Millennium Alert After Action Review and his classified notes.

- On October 2, 2003, after reviewing copies of NSC numbered documents, copies of Staff Member Office Files, and copies of e-mail documents, Berger again removed classified documents from the Archives. He admitted to removing numbered e-mail documents. Berger also removed the classified notes he took. Berger admitted he also temporarily left highly classified documents at a construction site where they could have been found by anyone.

- On these four occasions, Archives officials allowed Sandy Berger to review highly classified documents outside of a Sensitive Compartmented Information Facility. On several occasions, Berger deliberately procured the absence of Archives staff so that he could conceal and remove classified documents.

- Failure to engage law enforcement at the appropriate time compromised a proper investigation. Archives staff failed to notify law enforcement officials when there was a reasonable suspicion classified government property had been removed by Berger.

- The Archives Inspector General and Justice Department officials clashed over notifying the 9/11 Commission of the extent of Berger's document removal and the fact that Berger had access to original documents that may have been responsive to Commission document requests. No one told the 9/11 Commission that Berger had access to original documents.

- There is no basis for concluding Berger did not remove original documents responsive to 9/11 Commission requests during the May 30, 2002 and July 18, 2003 visits to the National Archives. Nevertheless, the Justice Department's representations to the 9/11 Commission left the impression that Berger's document theft was limited to what he admitted to taking.

- The public statements of the former chief of the Justice Department's Public Integrity Section, Noel Hillman, were incomplete and misleading. Because Berger had access to original documents on May 30, 2002, and July 18, 2003, there is no basis for his statement that "nothing was lost to the public or the process."

- The 9/11 Commission relied on assurances from the Department of Justice that a full and complete production was made, and that no original or any other responsive documents were withheld. No one told the 9/11 Commission that Berger had access to original documents. The 9/11 Commission was specifically interested in the office files of White House terrorism advisor Richard Clarke, and never was told that Berger had access to Clarke's original office files on May 30, 2002, and July 18, 2003.

III. Background

A. The National Archives

Established by statute in 1934[1], the National Archives and Records Administration is an independent agency charged with maintaining and protecting the records of the Federal Government.[2]

The retention of Presidential records is governed by the Presidential Records Act (PRA) of 1978 and Executive Order 13233.[3] The Act provides that all official Presidential and Vice Presidential records created after January 20, 1981 are the property of the Federal Government and establishes the legal basis for access to the records of Presidents, beginning with the Reagan administration.[4] Upon the conclusion of a President's term, the Archivist of the United States assumes responsibility for the custody, control, preservation of, and access to the Presidential records.[5]

B. 9/11 Commission

The National Commission on Terrorist Attacks Upon the United States (9/11 Commission), was an independent commission created by an act of Congress and signed into law by President George W. Bush in 2002. The 9/11 Commission was chartered to prepare a full and complete account of the circumstances surrounding the September 11,

---

[1] 44 U.S.C. §§2101-2118 (2000).

[2] Nat'l Archives and Records Admin. [hereinafter NARA], Ready Access to Essential Evidence, 2006 Performance and Accountability Rep., (2006), http://www.archives.gov/about/plans-reports/performance-accountability/2006/par2006-summary.pdf.

[3] 44 U.S.C. §§ 2201-2207 (2000); Exec. Order No. 13233 (2001).

[4] The Nat'l Archives, Presidential Libraries, http://www.archives.gov/presidential-libraries/laws/1978-act.html (last visited Jan. 5, 2007).

[5] 44 U.S.C. § 2203(f)(1).

2001 terrorist attacks on the United States, including preparedness for and the immediate response to the attacks.[6]

On July 22, 2004, the Commission released its Final Report. The Commission ceased operations on August 21, 2004.[7] The documents used and created by the 9/11 Commission are federal records and are maintained by the National Archives.

C. Sandy Berger

During President Clinton's second term, Samuel R. (Sandy) Berger was Assistant to the President for National Security Affairs, a position commonly known as the National Security Advisor.[8] Berger served President Clinton as National Security Advisor from March 14, 1997 to January 20, 2001.[9]

The National Security Advisor is a principal to the National Security Council (NSC), and oversees the NSC staff within the White House.[10]

> The National Security Council is the President's principal forum for considering national security and foreign policy matters with his senior national security advisors and cabinet officials. Since its inception under President Truman, the function of the Council has been to advise and assist the President on national security and foreign policies. The Council also serves as the President's principal arm for coordinating these policies among various government agencies.[11]

Berger's misconduct occurred as he was reviewing highly classified documents at the National Archives while preparing to represent President Clinton's NSC staff before the 9/11 Commission.

---

[6] The Comm'n on Terrorist Attacks Upon the U.S. [hereinafter The 9/11 Comm'n], http://www.9-11commission.gov/about/index.htm (last visited Jan. 5, 2007).

[7] The 9/11 Comm'n, http://www.9-11commission.gov/ (last visited Jan. 5, 2007).

[8] NARA, Nat'l Sec. Council Biography of Samuel R. Berger, http://clinton4.nara.gov/WH/EOP/NSC/html/bergerbio.html.

[9] White H. website, http://www.whitehouse.gov/nsc/history.html#summary, Appendix, Assistants to the President for Nat'l Security Affairs, 1953-1997.

[10] White H. website, Nat'l Security Council, http://www.whitehouse.gov/nsc/ (last visited Jan. 5, 2007).

[11] *Id.*

D. Criminal Investigation, Prosecution, and Guilty Plea

On October 10, 2003, the Inspector General of the National Archives (Archives IG) was advised that Berger removed classified documents from the Archives.[12] After a preliminary investigation, on October 15, 2003 the Archives IG referred the matter to the Department of Justice for criminal investigation.[13] The Department accepted the criminal referral and requested the Archives IG temporarily suspend its internal investigation pending the criminal investigation and prosecution of Berger.[14] On April 14, 2004, Justice Department officials advised the Archives IG's office it could resume its investigation with specific limitations on the witnesses with which the IG was permitted to speak.[15] On April 1, 2005, Berger pleaded guilty to one misdemeanor count of Unauthorized Removal and Retention of Classified Documents, in violation of 18 U.S.C. § 1924(a).[16]

On September 8, 2005, Magistrate Judge Deborah A. Robinson sentenced Berger to two years probation, 100 hours of community service, a $50,000 fine, and revoked his security clearance for three years.[17] Judge Robinson's sentence was much more costly to Berger than that recommended by the Department of Justice.[18] The Justice Department initially had proposed a fine of $10,000.[19] Judge Robinson stated, "The court finds the fine is inadequate because it doesn't reflect the seriousness of the offense."[20]

---

[12] Rep. of Investigations, Office of Inspector Gen. [hereinafter OIG], Office of Investigations, NARA, Case No.: 04-001-GC (Apr., 2005), at 15 [hereinafter IG Report].

[13] *Id.*

[14] *Id.*

[15] *Id.*

[16] Factual Basis for Plea at ¶3, *U.S. v. Samuel R. Berger,* No. CR-05-0175M-01 (D.D.C. Apr. 1, 2005) [hereinafter Berger, Factual Basis for Plea].

[17] Carol D. Leonnig, *Berger Is Fined For Smuggling Classified Papers,* WASH. POST, Sept. 9, 2005, at A7.

[18] Jerry Seper, *Berger Fined For Taking Papers; Judge Boosts Cost To $50,000,* WASH. TIMES, Sept. 9, 2005, at A1.

[19] *Id.*

[20] *Id.*

E. The Committee's Investigation

In August 2004, pursuant to the Committee's jurisdictional authority over the National Archives, it commenced an investigation into allegations that former National Security Advisor Sandy Berger improperly removed highly classified documents from the Archives.[21] The unauthorized removal of such documents raised serious questions about the procedures at the Archives for safeguarding these documents and specific questions as to whether the 9/11 Commission received all documents responsive to its document requests.

After consultation with the Department of Justice and the Archives IG's office, the Committee's investigation was held in abeyance while the Justice Department pursued criminal charges, and to allow an internal investigation by the IG. The IG completed work in November 2005 and issued a Report of Investigation. Following the Archives IG Report, the Committee's investigation remained in abeyance as the agency considered personnel action with respect to the relevant employees. The internal personnel review, actions, and subsequent appeals continued into October 2006. At the conclusion of these personnel inquiries in October 2006, the Committee resumed its investigation. Around the same time, on October 11, 2006, then Committee Chairman Tom Davis received a letter from 10 members of Congress, including then House Armed Services Committee Chairman Duncan Hunter and Judiciary Committee Chairman F. James Sensenbrenner, Jr., asking Chairman Davis to further investigate the Berger matter.[22]

Interviews were conducted with officials from the National Archives, the Office of Inspector General for the National Archives, the 9/11 Commission, the Department of Justice, and the Office of Inspector General for the Department of Justice. Noel Hillman, a former Justice Department official, declined to be interviewed. The Committee requested an interview with Sandy Berger. Through his lawyer, Lanny Breuer, Berger declined to be interviewed.

---

[21] Letter from Tom Davis, Chairman, H. Comm. on Gov't Reform [hereinafter Gov't Reform Comm.], to John W. Carlin, Archivist of the U.S., NARA (August 5, 2004) (on file with Gov't Reform Comm.); The Committee's jurisdictional authority over the National Archives is contained in Rule X(h)(7) of the Rules of the House of Representatives, 109th Cong. (2005).

[22] Letter from Reps. John L. Mica, Dan Burton, Daniel E. Lungren, Mark E. Souder, Patrick T. McHenry, F. James Sensenbrenner, Lynn A. Westmoreland, John J. Duncan, Jr., Curt Weldon, and Duncan Hunter to Tom Davis, Chairman, Gov't Reform Comm. (October 11, 2006) (on file with Gov't Reform Comm.).

IV. Berger's Four Visits

A. Designation by President Clinton

On April 12, 2002, President Clinton designated Berger as his representative to review NSC documents and prepare testimony for the Joint Intelligence Committee (Graham-Goss Commission) regarding its inquiry into Osama bin Laden, Al Qaeda, and other terrorism-related matters.[23] That designation led to Berger's involvement as a Clinton administration representative in reviewing documents responsive to the 9/11 Commission's requests.[24]

Pursuant to the Presidential Records Act, the 9/11 Commission's document requests relating to the Clinton administration were coordinated through the incumbent Executive Office of the President, the equity holder of the NSC documents.[25] For the Clinton years, numbered document requests were made to the Executive Office of the President, identified as numbered EOP requests, such as EOP 1, EOP 2 and EOP 3. In responding to the 9/11 Commission requests, officials from the National Archives' Presidential Materials Staff reviewed the Presidential records for responsive documents.[26]

While documents contained in the Staff Member Office Files were uninventoried originals, the NSC numbered documents were inventoried at the document level and organized in an archival database. NSC documents from the Clinton administration were transferred to the National Archives accompanied with an electronic records management system which serves as a basic index to the collection.[27] As a result, each document was given a seven-digit identifying number.[28] The document summary from the electronic records management system was used to locate the original version of the NSC document.[29]

---

[23] IG Report at 4.

[24] *Id.* at 3.

[25] *Id.* at 4.

[26] *Id.*

[27] Memorandum of Interview by Staff of OIG, NARA, with Billy "John" Laster, Presidential Materials Staff [hereinafter PMS], NARA, in Coll. Park, Md. (May 25, 2005), at 3 [hereinafter Laster Interview].; Memorandum of Interview by Staff of OIG, with John Laster, PMS, NARA, Kate Dillon-McClure, PMS, NARA, and Beth Fidler, PMS, NARA, Archives I, Wash., D.C. (May 31 – June 2, 2005), at 2 [hereinafter PMS Interview].

[28] Laster Interview at 3; PMS Interview at 2.

[29] Laster Interview at 3.

Archives staff reviewed the EOP document requests and established a list of search terms to identify all responsive documents for Berger to review.[30] Relevant documents also were suggested by the incumbent administration's NSC.[31] After culling all the potentially responsive documents, the documents were further reviewed by Archives staff for a final determination of responsiveness.[32] After the universe of potentially responsive documents was identified, representatives from the Clinton administration were provided access to the documents – originals in many cases – for a Presidential privilege review.[33]

The representatives for the Clinton administration were Sandy Berger and former Deputy National Security Advisor Nancy Soderberg.[34] After these individuals determined if any responsive document could be withheld on the basis that it a was privileged presidential communication, the National Archives forwarded the responsive documents to the incumbent NSC for final review. They were then submitted to the 9/11 Commission.[35]

Sandy Berger visited the National Archives to review Presidential records on four occasions. Berger reviewed documents in the office of Nancy Smith, Director of Presidential Materials Staff. The first visit, May 30, 2002, was in advance of his testimony before the Graham-Goss Commission. The subsequent three visits related to the 9/11 Commission document production, and in preparation for interviews with Commission staff and public testimony before the Commission.[36] The three 9/11 Commission-related visits occurred on July 18, September 2, and October 2, 2003.[37]

---

[30] *Id.*

[31] PMS Interview at 5.

[32] *Id.* at 4-6.

[33] IG Report at 3-4; PMS Interview at 6; Memorandum of Interview by Staff of OIG, with Nancy Keegan Smith, Dir. of PMS, NARA, in Wash., D.C. (Sept. 7-8, 2004), at 4 [hereinafter Smith Interview I].

[34] IG Report at 3-4; Smith Interview I at 4.

[35] IG Report at 4; Smith Interview I at 4.

[36] Memorandum of Interview by Staff of OIG, with Samuel R. Berger, former Nat'l Security Advisor to President William J. Clinton, in Wash., D.C. (July 8, 2005), at 2 [hereinafter Berger Interview].

[37] Berger, Factual Basis for Plea.

The majority of the materials Berger reviewed were highly classified Sensitive Compartmented Information and Special Access Program documents.[38]

B. Highly Classified Materials

During the relevant period, and before to the establishment of the position of the Director of National Intelligence in 2005, the Director of Central Intelligence had the authority for the establishment of intelligence policies for agencies such as the National Archives. These policies were formalized through Director of Central Intelligence Directives (DCIDs).[39] Unless rescinded or superseded by the National Intelligence Director through Intelligence Community Directives, DCIDs remain in force.[40]

Sensitive Compartmented Information (SCI) "is classified information concerning or derived from intelligence sources, methods, or analytical processes, which is required to be handled within formal access control systems established by the Director of Central Intelligence."[41]

SCI material must be stored within an accredited Sensitive Compartmented Information Facility (SCIF).[42] The Director of Central Intelligence is charged with accrediting SCIFs for executive branch departments and agencies outside the intelligence community, such as, the National Archives.[43] SCI material must be reviewed, processed, handled, and discussed in an accredited SCIF.[44]

Special Access Program (SAP) materials relate to any program which imposes need-to-know or access controls beyond those normally required for access to

---

[38] Laster Interview at 2.

[39] Nat'l Security Act of 1947, 50 U.S.C. §§ 401-442 (1947); Exec. Order No. 12333 (1981); Exec. Order No. 12958 (1995).

[40] Office of the Dir. of Nat'l Intelligence, Intelligence Cmty Policy Memorandum, No. 2006-100-1, at 3 (2006).

[41] Dir. of Cent. Intelligence Directive [hereinafter DCID] 1/19, Sec. Policy for Sensitive Compartmented Info. and Sec. Policy Manual, [hereinafter DCID 1/19] at 1.1.18 (Mar. 1, 1995); Exec. Order No. 12333 (1981); Exec. Order No. 12958 (1995).

[42] DCID 1/19 at 3.0; Exec. Order No. 12333 (1981); Exec. Order No. 12958 (1995).

[43] DCID 1/19 at 3.2.

[44] DCID 6/9, Physical Sec. Standards for Sensitive Compartmented Info. Facilities, at 2.3.2 (Nov. 18, 2002).

Confidential, Secret, or Top Secret information.[45] SAPs are established in circumstances where normal management and safeguarding procedures are not sufficient to limit need-to-know or access, and the number of persons who need access will be reasonably small and commensurate with the objective of providing extra protection for the information involved.[46] Special Access Programs are assigned a classified code word, or an unclassified nickname, or both.[47] To be cleared into a SAP program, an individual has to hold a minimum of four SCI clearances.[48]

At the National Archives, the procedures for safeguarding and handling classified information are contained in the Archives' Information Security manual, known with the agency, as the "Red Book."[49] The Red Book, last updated in 1989, is supplemented from time to time with "Interim Guidance" memoranda from Archives officials.[50]

At the conclusion of the Clinton presidency, the administration's records were transferred to the National Archives and placed under the supervision of the Presidential Materials Staff.[51] The Clinton records are stored in both Little Rock, Arkansas at the William J. Clinton Presidential Library, and in Washington, D.C. at the National Archives main facility.[52] The materials stored in Washington contain the Clinton administration's classified intelligence files, specifically 153 boxes, designated as the "W" intelligence files.[53] The W files included Sensitive Compartmented Information (SCI) and National Security Council-controlled Special Access Program (SAP)

---

[45] Exec. Order No. 12958 (1995); See also, Army Regulation 380-381, Special Access Programs and Sensitive Activities.

[46] Exec. Order No. 12958 (1995); See also, Army Regulation 380-381, Special Access Programs and Sensitive Activities.

[47] Exec. Order No. 12958 (1995); See also, Army Regulation 380-381, Special Access Programs and Sensitive Activities.

[48] Smith Interview I at 13.

[49] Info. Sec. Manual 202 (1989) at ¶¶ 2, 5 [hereinafter Red Book].

[50] See, e.g., Lewis J. Bellardo, Deputy Archivist of the U.S. and Chief of Staff, NARA, Interim Guidance 1600-5, Access to Materials Containing Classified Info. in NARA Research Rooms by Non-Governmental Persons (Mar. 31, 2004).

[51] IG Report at 3.

[52] *Id.*

[53] During times relevant to the Berger matter, the Archives had possession of 153 boxes. An additional box was added after the last Berger visit on Oct. 2, 2003; See Laster Interview at 2; PMS Interview at 1.

materials.[54] According to the Archives IG's interview memorandum, Smith "commented all items reviewed for the EOP requests were considered to contain some documentation classified at the SAP level."[55]

The material contained in the 153 boxes included National Security Council (NSC) numbered documents and Staff Member Office Files (SMOFs).[56]

The National Security Council numbered documents have a cover sheet with a classification stamp.[57] The numbering scheme reflects the year the document was prepared, the sensitivity level, and a sequential numerical identifier.[58] NSC numbered documents come in various forms, some with attachments. These documents do not contain page numbers and are not inventoried by Archives staff.[59] Accordingly, if attachments or specific pages within a NSC numbered document were removed but the base document and cover page remained, Archives staff would have no way to know that these portions were missing.[60]

Staff Member Office Files (SMOFs) contain the papers of individual White House staff.[61] SMOFs include a variety of papers, such as, draft NSC numbered documents, memos, e-mails, and handwritten notes, among other items.[62] These files are not inventoried by the Archives. Rather, there is only a log of what folders exist. Consequently, had Berger removed papers from a SMOF, it would be almost impossible for the Archives staff to know.

At the Archives, only four staff members within the Presidential Materials Staff had the requisite security clearances to handle and view the SAP W files.[63] Sandy Berger was the only approved person from the Clinton administration with the required clearances to review the files. Berger's former Deputy Nancy Soderberg was cleared to

---

[54] Laster Interview at 2.

[55] Smith Interview I at 4.

[56] PMS Interview at 1.

[57] *Id* at 2.

[58] *Id.*

[59] *Id.*

[60] *Id.*

[61] *Id.*

[62] *Id.*

[63] IG Report at 4.

view some SCI material, and Steven Naplin, a former staffer to Berger at the NSC, was cleared to the lower top secret clearance level.[64]

C. First Visit – May 30, 2002

FINDING: ***On May 30, 2002, Sandy Berger reviewed original NSC numbered documents and original Staff Member Office Files, including the office files of White House terrorism advisor Richard Clarke. After receiving document requests from the 9/11 Commission in 2003, Archives staff made available the same original document files Berger reviewed in May 2002.***

Berger came to the National Archives on May 30, 2002 to review documents in preparation for his testimony before the Graham-Goss Commission, a Congressional panel comprised of members of the House and Senate intelligence committees, charged with looking into the 9/11 terrorist attacks.[65]

On that visit, Berger reviewed materials in Smith's office at the main National Archives facility.[66] Smith prepared the documents for Berger's review and also supervised Berger during the review.[67] According to Smith, Berger reviewed three boxes of NSC W files, and he examined original NSC numbered documents and original Staff Member Office Files.[68] The Staff Member Office Files Berger reviewed contained original documents.

According to the Archives staff, on that visit, Berger was especially interested in White House terrorism advisor Richard Clarke's personal office files.[69] Clarke's files

---

[64] Nancy Kegan Smith Report, Dir. of PMS, NARA, Special Access Visits of Samuel Berger, a Designated Agent of President Clinton's at NARA's Presidential Materials Staff for Reviewing Materials Deemed Responsive to Two White H. Requests for Access to the Comm'n on Terrorism, [hereinafter Smith Report] (Oct. 24, 2003), at 1, 4; Laster Interview at 2.

[65] Thomas H. Kean & Lee H. Hamilton, Without Precedent: The Inside Story of the 9/11 Comm'n at 16 (2006) [hereinafter Kean & Hamilton].

[66] Smith Report at 2; IG Report at 4.

[67] Smith Report at 2.

[68] *Id.* According to Nancy Smith's staff, however, Berger reviewed five boxes of materials. The Archives IG reported the staff supplied Berger with one box of NSC numbered documents and four boxes of Staff Member Office Files. PMS Interview at 3.

[69] *Id.*

were contained in box W-049.[70] The materials from this visit were among the first documents identified by Archives staff as responsive to 9/11 Commission requests.[71] Except for lunch, Berger spent the entire day at the Archives.[72] During the document review, Berger took handwritten notes.[73] Pursuant to conditions of reviewing classified documents, Berger's notes were to be left behind, and forwarded to the NSC for classification.[74] Berger claimed that he complied with these rules on May 30 when he left notes which were later forwarded by Archives staff to NSC for classification.[75] Following classification, the notes were returned to the Archives.[76]

D. Second Visit – July 18, 2003

FINDING: *On July 18, 2003, after reviewing original NSC numbered documents and original Staff Member Office Files, Sandy Berger removed the classified notes he took on that visit.*

According to Smith, Berger visited the National Archives on July 18, 2003 to review five boxes of documents responsive to the EOP 2 request from the 9/11 Commission.[77] The staff interview notes prepared by the Archives IG state that Berger was only provided four boxes; three boxes of Staff Member Office Files, and one box containing NSC numbered documents.[78] These materials were reviewed in Nancy Smith's office.[79] According to the Archives IG report, during that visit, Berger reviewed original NSC numbered documents, and original Staff Member Office Files.[80] According to Smith, for a large part of that visit, Smith sat at a table with Berger reviewing each item for relevancy.[81] In her report, Smith raised some issues with the manner in which

[70] *Id.*

[71] *Id* at 4.

[72] Smith Report at 2.

[73] *Id.*

[74] *Id.*

[75] *Id.*

[76] *Id.*

[77] *Id.* at 3; Laster Interview at 3.

[78] PMS Interview at 4.

[79] Smith Report at 3.

[80] IG Report at 5.

[81] Smith Report at 3.

Berger reviewed the documents on the July 18 visit.[82] "I did not like the way Mr. Berger archivally handled the records, ie (sic) sometimes he was not clear as to where to refile a tabbed item; so as the day continued, I checked what he had been through to make sure the folders and documents were in good order."[83] She stated, "Mr. Berger did voice on this visit that he would prefer to see the items in chronological order if that was at all possible."[84]

Smith told the Archives IG that Berger believed he was rushed and indicated some disgust with the burden and responsibility of conducting the document review.[85]

According to an account of his interview prepared by Archives IG investigators, Berger was advised by Smith that all notes he took during his document review were to be retained by the Archives.[86] Berger, however, admittedly removed his handwritten notes on three of his four visits to the Archives.[87]

According to the Archives IG's interview report, Berger realized during his document review that he needed to remove his notes from the Archives.[88] The report stated: "He realized he was not going to be able to reconstruct in detail all the documents he had reviewed, so he needed to take his notes with him, about ten to twenty pages."[89] The Archives IG's interview notes further state:

> At the end of the day, Mr. Berger tri-folded his notes and put them in his suit pocket. He took the opportunity to do this when Ms. Smith was out of her office due to him being on a private phone call. Mr. Berger said he did not recall being hesitant to remove his suit jacket during this visit. However, at some point, him not removing his jacket could have been related to the fact he placed the notes in his jacket. Mr. Berger knew he had to leave some notes behind so it would not be obvious he removed notes. He had been making notes and if he did not leave any behind it would have been noticeable.

---

[82] *Id.*

[83] *Id.*

[84] *Id.*

[85] Smith Interview I at 5.

[86] Berger Interview at 2.

[87] *Id.* at 4, 5, 7.

[88] *Id.* at 3.

[89] *Id.*

The Archives IG investigators' notes state that Berger was surprised to learn that he left only two pages of handwritten notes.[90] Berger reportedly told the IG investigators "some notes were better than none."[91]

E. Third Visit – September 2, 2003

> **FINDING:** *On September 2, 2003, after reviewing original NSC numbered documents, copies of Staff Member Office Files, and copies of e-mail documents, Sandy Berger removed classified documents from the Archives. He admitted to removing a classified version of the Millennium Alert After Action Review and his classified notes.*

To review documents responsive to EOP 3, Berger visited the Archives on September 2, 2003.[92] For that visit, Archives staff photocopied Staff Member Office File materials and placed them in chronological order to satisfy Berger's request from the July 2003 visit.[93]

Berger reviewed this material, in addition to original NSC numbered documents, in Smith's office at the main Archives building.[94] The Archives IG reported that Archives staff provided Berger three folders containing materials from Staff Member Office Files, one redwell containing NSC numbered documents, and printed e-mails deemed responsive to EOP 3.[95] During that visit, according to Smith, Berger "was difficult to deal with including demanding that I leave my office on several occasions so that he could make or take private phone calls."[96]

One document reviewed by Berger on September 2 was in response to EOP 2.[97] Shortly after Berger's July 18 visit, staff from the Clinton Library faxed a document to

---

[90] *Id.* at 4.

[91] *Id.*

[92] Smith Report at 4.

[93] *Id.* at 3-4.

[94] *Id.* at 4.

[95] PMS Interview at 6.

[96] Smith Report at 4.

[97] *Id.* at 10.

the Archives (hereinafter "Little Rock Fax"), after discovering code-worded classified materials were stored in Little Rock.[98] Smith advised staff in Little Rock that the code worded document was to be stored in Washington at the Archives.[99] The fax was transmitted over a secure telephone unit (STU) in accordance with relevant procedures.[100] After reviewing the Little Rock Fax in July, Smith determined it was to be reviewed by Berger on his next visit.[101] That occurred on the September 2 visit.[102] The Little Rock Fax later proved to be one of the documents removed by Berger.[103]

The Little Rock Fax was a version of the Millennium Alert After Action Review drafted by White House terrorism advisor Richard Clarke.[104] Following the arrest of Ahmed Ressam, who had planned acts of terrorism at Los Angeles International Airport on December 31, 1999.[105] Berger had asked Clarke to prepare an after-action review to identify national vulnerabilities.[106] In his March 24, 2004 public testimony to the 9/11 Commission, Berger said he had ordered the review, and Clarke's report contained 29 recommendations, most related to funding specific initiatives.[107] Clarke's report, for example, led President Clinton to request $300 million in funding from Congress for domestic security programs.[108]

The Archives IG investigators recounted what Berger told them about removing the Little Rock Fax:

> Mr. Berger took the first opportunity when Ms. Smith was out of her office to remove the document. He most likely put it in his

---

[98] *Id.*

[99] *Id.*

[100] *Id.*

[101] *Id.*

[102] *Id.*

[103] *Id.*

[104] Berger Interview at 5.

[105] The 9/11 Comm'n, Final Rep. of the Nat'l Comm'n on Terrorist Attacks Upon the U.S. [hereinafter The 9/11 Report] 176-79 (2004).

[106] Berger Interview at 5.

[107] Susan Schmidt and Dan Eggen, *FBI Probes Berger*, WASH. POST, July 20, 2004, at A2.

[108] *Id.*

jacket pocket, after folding it, but he does not have a precise recollection of where he put the document. It is perceivable he put it in his pants pocket. It was also possible he placed it in his portfolio and took it out. The document was twelve to thirteen pages.[109]

A peculiar incident occurred during the September 2 visit. A member of the Presidential Materials Staff – one of the four staff members with the required security clearances to handle the W files – reported suspicious activity by Berger to Smith.[110] In an e-mail to Smith, this staff member wrote:

> Okay, I know this is odd. He walked out the door in front of me and into the hallway. The door closed. Shortly after it closed, I proceeded to go get him a Diet Coke. When I opened the door and started down the hall, he was stooped over right outside the doorway. He was fiddling with something white which looked to be a piece of paper or multiple pieces of paper. It appeared to be rolled around his ankle and underneath his pant leg, with a portion of the paper sticking out underneath.
>
> He turned his head toward my direction as I went by him. We did not make eye contact.
>
> I can't be 100 percent sure of what I saw because it happened so quickly. But there was clearly something there more than his pants and socks.[111]

In his interview with the Archives IG, Laster's account is explained as follows:

> Mr. Laster's office is in the next suite from Ms. Smith's. Ms. Smith stepped out of her office asked (sic) Mr. Laster to buy her and Mr. Berger a diet coke (sic). Mr. Laster got up and headed towards the reception area. Mr. Berger stepped out of Ms. Smith's office and out of the suite. Mr. Laster came out of the suite and had to side step Mr. Berger so he would not run into him. Mr. Laster noticed the (sic) Mr. Berger was fiddling with something around his left ankle, between his sock and his pant leg. It could have been paper. Mr. Berger was bent over or crouched down, possibly on one knee. His pant leg was pulled up around his calf

---

[109] Berger Interview at 5.

[110] Smith Report at 4.

[111] E-mail from John Laster, PMS, NARA to Nancy Smith, Dir. of PMS, NARA (Sept. 2, 2003, 5:58 p.m. EST) (on file with Gov't Reform Comm.).

area. The white material extended beyond the hem of Mr. Berger's pant leg. Mr. Laster said that he could see Mr. Berger's sock below, and underneath, the white material. The white material was around Mr. Berger's sock, not in it. It was an odd place to see something white on someone. The white material had more of an appearance of paper than fabric. Mr. Laster was 100 percent sure the white material was not Mr. Berger's skin. It all happened very quickly.[112]

In her report, Smith stated, "I was concerned by what John told me."[113] She speculated that Berger may have been suffering from a health problem, possibly phlebitis.[114] Those suffering from phlebitis sometimes don prescription leg compression stockings.

Although Berger reviewed copies of e-mails during the September 2 visit, one member of the Archives staff explained to the Archives IG that had Berger removed copies of the e-mails, it would be very difficult to re-locate or re-create the e-mail because of the labor intensive process of identifying the responsive e-mail documents.[115] In response to the 9/11 Commission EOP document requests, Archives staff searched the electronically stored e-mails for a list of pre-identified search terms or key words.[116] Once an e-mail was identified as potentially responsive by the staff, a single print was made and passed on to Smith. She provided it to Berger.[117] Since no other print-outs were made, if an e-mail was removed from the document collection, Berger could have prevented the 9/11 Commission from having access to it.[118]

---

[112] Laster Interview at 4-5.

[113] Smith Report at 4.

[114] *Id.*

[115] PMS Interview at 7.

[116] *Id.*

[117] *Id.*

[118] *Id.*

F. Fourth Visit – October 2, 2003

FINDING: *On October 2, 2003, after reviewing copies of NSC numbered documents, copies of Staff Member Office Files, and copies of e-mail documents, Berger again removed classified documents from the Archives. He admitted to removing numbered e-mail documents. Berger also removed the classified notes he took. Berger admitted he also temporarily left highly classified documents at a construction site where they could have been found by anyone.*

Berger visited the Archives on October 2, 2003 to complete the review of documents responsive to EOP 3. The document review also occurred in Smith's office.[119] On that date, Berger arrived at 11:30 a.m. and departed at 7 p.m., without taking a lunch break.[120] Because of the concerns raised by John Laster's e-mail during the September 2 visit, Berger was only provided with copies of NSC numbered documents, copies of Staff Member Office Files, print-out copies of e-mails, copies of Steven Naplan's notes, and a document identified by Naplan as one that Berger needed to examine before it was produced.[121] In total, on October 2, Berger reviewed one box of e-mail documents and one box containing the NSC numbered documents and SMOF materials.[122] These documents were reviewed by Berger one redwell at a time.[123]

Smith and her staff took the additional step of numbering each document that was reviewed by Berger.[124] Smith penciled a number on the reverse side of each document.[125] When Berger left Smith's office to visit the men's room, Smith examined the documents he had reviewed and verified that no numbered documents were missing.[126] The Archives IG reported that John Laster of the Presidential Materials Staff observed what he considered "agitated" behavior by Berger.[127] The Archives IG's interview notes of

---

[119] Smith Report at 5.

[120] *Id.* at 5-6.

[121] *Id.* at 5; Laster Interview at 6.

[122] PMS Interview at 7.

[123] Laster Interview at 6.

[124] Smith Report at 5.

[125] *Id.*

[126] *Id.*

[127] Laster Interview at 7.

Laster stated, "Mr. Berger visited the bathroom more frequently than he had on previous visits. Especially considering that he did not have much to drink."[128] The interview notes prepared following Berger's interview by the Archives IG stated that he acknowledged visiting the restroom every 30 minutes as a general practice.[129]

During one of Berger's afternoon restroom visits, Archives staff determined that an e-mail was missing.[130] After conferring with her staff, Smith had another copy printed and placed in with the document set Berger was in the process of reviewing.[131] At the time, Smith and her staff concluded that it was possible that there was a numbering error, and no document number 217 ever existed.[132] Her report stated:

> They [her staff] gave me the e-mail, which were (sic) number 217. I brought it in to Berger and stated that apparently when we had provided e-mail this number had been skipped, that we had a way of controlling the e-mails and that we had noticed that this number was absent from what he had returned. Berger looked at the e-mail and said he was sure he had seen this e-mail and that it must be included already. He asked me if I did not remember seeing it? I said that I had knew I had seen similar information, but that this unique e-mail number was missing, that the archives considers each separate e-mail a unique record unless it is totally duplicative in its information, and that he need (sic) to look at this e-mail because we needed to provide it as a separate document. About 5 minutes later, Berger said he was sorry but that had (sic) to make a private phone call and demanded that I leave the office. Reluctantly, I did leave, but checked [a colleague's] phone which is right outside of my office and noticed that no phone conversation was going on. I also remembered at the beginning of the day that Berger had said that his cell phone was not working. So I immediately returned to my office at which point I almost ran into Berger who was going down to the bathroom again. He had just been a few minutes ago.[133]

---

[128] *Id.*

[129] Berger Interview at 2.

[130] Smith Report at 6.

[131] *Id.*

[132] *Id.*

[133] *Id.*

On October 3, Smith and her staff examined the documents Berger reviewed.[134] Smith's staff reported that three numbered e-mails were missing, including the document numbered 217.[135] Other missing numbers were 150 and 323.[136] The staff then recreated the e-mails that were missing.[137] According to Smith, they were all copies or drafts of the same highly classified Millennium Alert After Action Report.[138] The only difference among the missing documents were e-mail responses.[139] The missing documents were also the same base document (copies or drafts) as the Little Rock Fax.[140] Document number 150 was an e-mail with no content, just a subject line, and the attached after-action report.[141] Document number 217 contained three lines of e-mail text and the attachment.[142] Document number 323, contained three paragraphs of e-mail text and the attached report.[143]

Document number 150 was also mistakenly reviewed by Steve Naplan when he was reviewing top secret documents.[144] The SCI and SAP material Berger was reviewing was too highly classified for anyone without the high security clearances Berger had.[145] Naplan, however, was provided document number 150, during his review because of a misclassification error.[146] During the course of Naplan's review, he placed a pink sticker on the document with a note that Berger must review.[147]

---

[134] *Id.*; Laster Interview at 8.

[135] Smith Report at 6; Laster Interview at 8.

[136] *Id.*

[137] Smith Report at 6.

[138] *Id.*

[139] *Id.*

[140] Smith Report at 10.

[141] PMS Interview at 11.

[142] *Id.*

[143] *Id.*

[144] Smith Report at 6.

[145] *Id.*

[146] *Id.*

[147] *Id.*

After examining the documents Berger was provided, Smith and her staff knew that document number 150 was missing.[148] The pink sticker had been placed on document number 156.[149] By moving the pink sticker from document number 150 to 156, it appears Berger was carefully thinking through his document theft, knowing that if he failed to leave the pink-stickered document behind, he would be caught. In the report she prepared, Smith stated, "[m]y staff and I were almost physically ill with the discovery of missing e-mails."[150]

Although control sets were established for the NSC numbered documents and the SMOFs, a control set was not used for the e-mails reviewed by Berger.[151] When the staff suspected Berger had taken e-mail documents, they had to go back and recreate the search process based on the dates of document numbers 216 and 218.[152]

The process of relocating document number 217 was explained to the Archives IG by Archives staff.

> Ms. Fidler was reviewing the folders at someone's desk, outside Ms. Smith's office, when she discovered #217 missing. Mr. Laster believed he verified it was missing.
>
> Mr. Laster gave Ms. Dillon-McClure the date of the document before the missing email and the date of the document after the missing email, from email #216 and #218. This was the time frame in which Ms. Dillon-McClure searched the emails, using the same search terms which were responsive to the EOP request. The staff was able to verify there was an email that should have been printed and produced to Mr. Berger in that time frame. Ms. Dillon-McClure located the missing email. Ms. Dillon-McClure then left for the day, before printing the missing email. Ms. Dillon-McClure called back to the office to ensure Ms. Fidler knew what to look for on the email system in order to find the email in question. Ms. Fidler told Mr. Laster another copy of this email was printed, she wrote #217 on the back, and provided to Ms. Smiht (sic).[153]

---

[148] Smith Report at 7.

[149] *Id.* at 6-7; PMS Interview at 9.

[150] Smith Report at 7.

[151] PMS Interview at 8.

[152] *Id.*

[153] *Id.*

The interview notes prepared by the Archives IG following their interview with Berger stated:

> Ms. Smith first provided Mr. Berger the documents marked for review by Mr. Naplan. A version of the MAAR was with these documents, market SECRET. Mr. Berger did not know why it was classified differently than the version he removed in September which was TOP SECRET CODEWORD. It was obvious to him this was a different version of the MAAR. Mr. Clarke had mentioned the MAAR went through several iterations but the changes were over money not substantive (sic). Mr. Berger placed this version under his portfolio while Ms. Smith's assistant was in the office.

* * *

> About mid-day, Mr. Berger came across another version of the MAAR. . . . Mr. Berger saw a version of the MAAR and now had doubts that what he removed in September was the final report. At this point, he wanted to track the evolution of the MAAR. He slid the document under his portfolio.

> Ms. Smith told Mr. Berger there was a missing document, one that she could not find. Mr. Berger said at this point "the bomb should have burst in the air, but obviously it did not.

* * *

> Ms. Smith gave him another copy of the document. Mr. Berger slid this document under his portfolio also. Ms. Smith did not ask for it back. If she had asked for it back, it would have "triggered" a decision for him to give the documents back.[154]

At around 6 p.m., Berger expressed his desire to leave for the day.[155] Smith wanted Berger to stay and complete the review.[156] Smith suggested Berger take a walk and come back and finish up. What Berger did next is another bizarre and peculiar twist in the story. The Archives IG reported it as follows:

---

[154] Berger Interview at 6-7.

[155] *Id.* at 7.

[156] *Id.*

Mr. Berger left the building with all the documents he put in his pockets. He was aware of the risk he was taking, but he also knew the guards were not there in the evening.

Mr. Berger exited the Archives on to Pennsylvania Avenue, the north entrance. It was dark. He did not want to run the risk of bringing the documents back in the building risking the possibility Ms. Smith might notice something unusual. He headed towards a construction area on Ninth Street. Mr. Berger looked up and down the street, up into the windows of the Archives and the DOJ, and did not see anyone. He removed the documents from his pockets, folded the notes in a "V" shape and inserted the documents in the center. He walked inside the construction fence and slid the documents under a trailer.[157]

After leaving the Archives on October 2 and retrieving the documents left at the construction site, Berger told the IG's investigators that he went to his office and destroyed three of the documents he removed by cutting them into small pieces and disposed of them in his office trash can.[158] Berger's acknowledgement that he cut the documents into small pieces contradicted his statement made to the media in July 2004: "When I was informed by the Archives that there were documents missing, I immediately returned everything I had except for a few documents that I apparently had accidentally discarded."[159]

During his interview with Archives IG investigators, Berger admitted to removing four documents during the October 2 visit plus copies of his handwritten notes.[160] That brought his tally of admittedly removed documents to five – four from the October 2 visit, and one, the Little Rock Fax, from the September 2 visit. In addition, on all three of his 9/11 Commission-related visits, Berger also removed his personal handwritten notes, which because based on classified data, are automatically themselves classified.[161]

---

[157] *Id.*

[158] *Id.* at 8.

[159] John Solomon, *Clinton Advisor Probed for Taking Classified Terror Memos*, ASSOCIATED PRESS, July 19, 2004 [hereinafter Solomon July 19, 2004 article].

[160] Berger Interview at 7.

[161] *Id.* at 4, 5, 7; Exec. Order No. 12958 (1995), Part 2 Derivative Classification.

G. Berger Is Caught

On October 3, after concluding that documents were missing, Smith telephoned Archives General Counsel Gary Stern.[162] Smith also left a message for her supervisor, Richard Claypoole, who was out of town, to call her as soon as possible.[163] After being briefed by Smith, Stern contacted the then Archivist of the United States John Carlin.[164]

The next day, Saturday, October 4, after having been briefed by Stern, the Archivist contacted Smith to discuss the matter.[165] On the afternoon of October 4, Smith met with Stern and Steve Hannestead, Director of Space and Security for the Archives.[166] Not knowing precisely the best way to approach Berger about the matter, Smith, Stern, and Hannestead settled on contacting Bruce Lindsey.[167] After some back and forth between Lindsey and Berger, and then Lindsey and the Archives staff, the Archives contacted Berger directly.[168] According to Smith, Berger was insistent that he did not have the documents.[169] In her report, Smith writes of a conversation with Berger:

> He said that he remembered that e-mail well, because the topic was of interest to him and that he had been comparing several copies of it to try to find the most final copy. Berger said that he remembered turning in the e-mail that Steve Naplan had marked with the pink tab. I said that he did return a folder with an e-mail with a pink tab, but that when we checked the e-mail he had handed back in with the pink tab, it was not the right e-mail. I told Berger we could tell this because we had checked Steve Naplan's notes that had described the e-mail in detail by subject and date, and the e-mail that now had the pink tab on it did not match the note. The e-mail that Steve Naplan had tabbed had been numbered as 150 which was now missing and the tab was on a different numbered e-mail. Berger said perhaps in comparing the copies of

---

[162] Smith Report at 7.

[163] *Id.* at 7.

[164] *Id.* at 7.

[165] *Id.* at 7.

[166] *Id.* at 8.

[167] *Id.* at 8.

[168] *Id.* at 8.

[169] *Id.* at 8.

these e-mails to find the most final he made (sic) moved them out of order, but that is all he could think of. I said that we had already checked, that copies that we had served him of these three numbered e-mails were missing and could he please continue to look.

After the dinner hour on October 4, Berger called Smith, and according to Smith, implied that the Archives was responsible for losing the documents.[170] To this end, according to Smith, Berger advised "that we too should check" for the missing documents.[171] Reversing course, at approximately 11 p.m., Berger called Gary Stern, and according to Smith, notified Stern that he had "found" two documents.[172] Stern made arrangements with Berger to have the documents retrieved.[173]

On Sunday, October 5, Archives staff met Berger, and he returned document number 323 and the Little Rock Fax.[174] Also on Sunday, Archives staff notified personnel from the NSC, the equity holder of the documents.[175] A formal meeting with the NSC was scheduled for October 7.

On October 7, 2003, Archives staff met with NSC officials. At that meeting, NSC General Counsel John Bellinger advised Archives staff of the NSC's desire to have the matter handled by the Archives, the entity with legal custody of the documents.[176] Bellinger told the Archives staff that he had spoken with White House Counsel Alberto Gonzales, and Gonzales wanted the matter handled by the National Archives.[177] Bellinger also provided the Archives staff with the names of lawyers at the Department of Justice to contact regarding a formal criminal investigation.[178]

---

[170] *Id.* at 9.

[171] *Id.* at 9.

[172] *Id.* at 9.

[173] *Id.* at 9.

[174] *Id.* at 9.

[175] *Id.* at 10.

[176] *Id.* at 11.

[177] *Id.* at 11.

[178] *Id.* at 11.

On October 10, Archives staff was notified by Berger's lawyer, Lanny Breuer, that Berger had additional documents to return. Arrangements were made to pick up notes Berger took while at the Archives and that he had improperly removed.[179]

H. Berger's Public Statements

Berger's public statements months after the incident took place differ substantially from his later admissions. In an Associated Press article on July 19, 2004, Berger stated, "I inadvertently took a few documents from the Archives."[180]

This is false. Berger later admitted that he intentionally, and in a premeditated fashion, procured the absence of Smith, and hid the documents on his person, both in his pants pocket and his suit coat pocket. In the July 19 article, Berger lied when addressing whether he destroyed some of the documents he removed. He said, "When I was informed by the Archives that there were documents missing, I immediately returned everything I had except for a few documents that I apparently had accidentally discarded."[181]

This is also false. Berger had destroyed documents by cutting them into small pieces. His lawyer, Lanny Breuer, told the Associated Press for the July 19 article, that Berger believed he was looking at copies of documents.[182] This is false. Berger was provided with original documents on three of his four visits to the Archives, including original Staff Member Office File that contain personal handwritten notes and other obviously original materials that would be found in anyone's personal office files.

In a July 20 *Washington Post* story, Breuer stated, Berger's actions were the result of sloppiness and were unintentional.[183] As Berger later admitted, this proved untrue. In a July 22 *Washington Post* story, through spokesman Joe Lockhart, Berger continued to publicly depict the facts in a false manner. Assuming the role of the victim, Berger "also feels a sense of injustice that after building a reputation as a tireless defender of his

---

[179] *Id.* at 11.

[180] Solomon July 19, 2004 article.

[181] *Id.*

[182] *Id.*

[183] Susan Schmidt and Dan Eggen, *FBI Probes Berger for Document Removal; Former Clinton Aide Inadvertently Took Papers From Archives, His Attorney Says*, WASH. POST, July 20, 2004, at A2.

country that many Republicans would try to assassinate his character to pursue their own ends," Lockhart said.[184]

V. Lax Procedures at National Archives Created an Environment Where Berger Easily Removed Highly Classified Documents

A. Classified Documents Handled Inappropriately

FINDING: *On these four occasions, Archives officials allowed Sandy Berger to review highly classified documents outside of a Sensitive Compartmented Information Facility. On several occasions, Berger deliberately procured the absence of Archives staff so that he could conceal and remove classified documents.*

According to Jason Baron, the representative from the National Archives' General Counsel's office interviewed by Committee staff, Smith and her staff were under the mistaken impression that Smith's office was a CIA-designated Secure Working Area, and consequently, a permissible area to review classified documents.[185] This mistaken belief had held among Archives personnel perhaps since 1993, according to Baron.[186]

Pursuant to CIA directive, SCI material must be reviewed in a SCIF.[187] Director of Central Intelligence Directive 6/9 relating to Physical Security Standards for Sensitive Compartmented Information Facilities, section 2.3.2 states, "SCI shall never be handled, processed, discussed, or stored in any facility other than a properly accredited SCIF unless a written authorization is granted" by the appropriate security authority.[188] Executive Order 12958 on Classified Information specifies agency heads to "establish controls to ensure that classified information is used, processed, stored, reproduced,

---

[184] John F. Harris and Susan Schmidt, *Archives Staff Was Suspicious of Berger; Why Documents Were Missing Is Disputed*, WASH. POST, July 22, 2004, at A6 [hereinafter Harris/Schmidt July 22, 2004 article].

[185] Interview by Gov't Reform Comm. Staff with Jason R. Baron, Dir. of Litig., Office of the Gen. Counsel, NARA, in Wash., D.C. (Nov. 20, 2006) [hereinafter Baron Interview].

[186] Baron Interview.

[187] DCID 6/9 at 2.3.2; See also NARA, Interim Guidance 1600-5 (March 31, 2004).

[188] Memorandum of Interview by Staff of OIG, with Nancy Keegan Smith, Dir. of PMS, NARA, in Archives I, Coll. Park, Md. (Sept. 12, 2005), at 2 [hereinafter Smith Interview II]; Red Book references DCIDs (Chapter 2, part 1, pg. 2-5, no. 9a).

transmitted, and destroyed under conditions that provide adequate protection . . . . "[189] Updated Archives guidelines, as of March 2004, specify those reviewing classified materials are to "use a Sensitive Compartmented Information Facility (SCIF) or dedicated conference room or other limited-access area, not an active office."[190]

Each visit by Berger occurred in Smith's office in the main Archives facility in Washington, D.C.[191] Berger was not briefed by Smith about the procedures for reviewing the documents.[192] Berger believed he was afforded the opportunity to conduct the document review in Smith's office as it was a more comfortable room than the SCIF, which was described to him as a less comfortable work area.[193]

The records were brought from the SCIF to Smith's office for Berger's review.[194] According to Archives staff, despite it not being a CIA-approved SCIF, Smith's office was sometimes used to review SCI material.[195] The Archives IG reported, John Laster, a staff member on the Presidential Materials Staff, stated he "did not believe there were any issues with reviewing SCI material in Ms. Smith's office."[196] Laster claimed that SCI material could be viewed in Smith's office "as long as it was a controlled environment, the reviewer was monitored, and the reviewer had the appropriate clearances."[197] The notes prepared by the IG, however, are clear that Laster knew Smith's office was not a SCIF.[198] Cell phones, for example, Laster is reported to have said, were permissible in Smith's office, and not in the SCIF where the Presidential Materials Staff stored sensitive documents.[199] The Archives IG reported Laster said that Berger is not the only person to have reviewed sensitive documents in Smith's office.[200]

---

[189] Exec. Order No. 12958 (1995), Part 4 Safeguarding, §4.2(f).

[190] NARA Interim Guidance ¶4(b).

[191] Smith Report; Laster Interview at 2.

[192] Berger Interview at 2.

[193] *Id.*

[194] Laster Interview at 2.

[195] *Id.*; Baron Interview.

[196] Laster Interview at 2.

[197] *Id.*

[198] Laster Interview at 10.

[199] *Id.*

[200] Laster Interview at 3.

Others were two Clinton representatives – Nancy Soderberg, and Bruce Lindsey – and John Mince, President Reagan's representative.[201]

Berger also was permitted to bring his portfolio to Smith's office during his document review.[202] The Archives IG's interview notes prepared following an interview with Smith stated, "[m]ost officials reviewing documents in the SCIF were allowed to bring in brief cases, notebooks, and paper. She assumed because of the security clearances granted these individuals they were aware of the prohibition of cell phones in a SCIF."[203] Berger often procured Smith's absence, leaving him unmonitored for periods of time. While usually she was bullied into this, she told the IG it made her feel uncomfortable.[204] The Archives IG's interview notes stated:

> Mr. Berger would normally use her phone to make calls. Mr. Berger would say "Sorry, I have to make a private phone call" and Ms. Smith would take this as her cue to leave. Mr. Berger would normally use her phone to make calls. Ms. Smith left as she trusted Mr. Berger and was aware that Mr. Berger, as National Security Advisor, had generated most of the documents that he was reviewing. However, Ms. Smith did not like leaving her office. This was because she works with sensitive items of the incumbent President and did not feel comfortable leaving Mr. Berger alone with this material, especially on her desk where her phone was located.[205]

The interview notes prepared following Berger's interview with the Archives IG investigators concur. On the July 18, 2003 visit, for example, Berger reportedly stated that his secretary called him "half a dozen times."[206] The notes stated:

> Mr. Berger told Ms. Smith he was happy to go outside her office to take the calls. Ms. Smith asked Mr. Berger if he needed privacy to which he said 'yes.' Ms. Smith said instead that she would go outside her office while he was on the phone, which she did. Once

---

[201] *Id.*

[202] Smith Interview I at 4.

[203] *Id.*

[204] *Id.*

[205] Smith Interview I at 6.

[206] Berger Interview at 3.

this pattern was established, he thought the offer for her to leave her office was 'standing.'[207]

Baron confirmed to Committee staff that Berger was provided original documents in the form of Staff Member Office Files and NSC numbered documents during his first two visits to the Archives.[208] Likewise, Berger reviewed original NSC numbered documents on September 2, 2003.

The Archives cannot be certain that Berger did not remove documents during these first two visits.[209] Whole original documents from the SMOFs and parts of original numbered NSC documents – which are inventoried only by their cover page – could be removed without any way to detect their removal. Baron acknowledged that it is conceivable that the 9/11 Commission may not have received all documents responsive to the EOP document requests.[210] There is no way to verify that Berger did not remove original documents on May 30, 2002, July 18, 2003, and September 2, 2003.

B. After Breach, Law Enforcement Not Engaged Quickly

FINDING: *Failure to engage law enforcement at the appropriate time compromised a proper investigation. Archives staff failed to notify law enforcement officials when there was a reasonable suspicion classified government property had been removed by Berger.*

At the Archives, security procedures and requirements are contained in the Information Security Manual, also known as the "Red Book."[211] The Red Book, however, was last published in 1989.[212] Some at the Archives consider it out of date for

---

[207] *Id.*

[208] Telephonic Interview by Gov't Reform Comm. Staff with Jason R. Baron, Dir. of Litig., Office of the Gen. Counsel, NARA, in Wash., D.C. (Nov. 27, 2006) [hereinafter Baron Telephonic Interview].

[209] *Id.*

[210] *Id.*

[211] Baron Interview; Laster Interview at 10.

[212] Red Book.

reference purposes.[213]   Ms. Smith told the Archives IG the Red Book was out of date, and to this end, was in the process of being updated by the Archives.[214]

Under Red Book guidelines, if Archives personnel discover a possible compromise of classified information, they are required to notify the agency's security manager.[215] By notifying Archives General Counsel Gary Stern and Director of Space and Security Stephen Hannestad, Archives officials say they believe Smith complied with her Red Book obligations.[216] Archives officials maintain the Red Book only requires the Department of Justice to be notified when espionage is suspected.[217] The Archives IG concluded that since espionage could not be ruled out, Justice Department officials should have been notified immediately.[218]

Smith was familiar with the Director of Central Intelligence Directives (DCIDs) but believed their reach extended only to agencies formally within the intelligence community.[219] Since the National Archives is not part of the intelligence community, its applicability to Archives personnel was not clear to Smith.[220] Had they been applicable to the Archives, Smith told the Archives IG, she thought they would have been incorporated into the Red Book.[221] According to the Archives IG's Report, the Red Book does reference and incorporate the DCIDs.[222]

Archives officials made a terrible mistake in not notifying law enforcement officials, which has serious consequences for the integrity of the Archives documents. Immediate notification in response to suspicions that Berger had stolen classified documents may have allowed for the government to retrieve the materials Berger removed. Whether espionage is a motive for removing classified materials or not, law enforcement should have been notified. The purpose of classified document control is national security broadly, not only counter-espionage. The ad hoc inquiries by Archives

---

[213] Laster Interview at 10.

[214] Smith Interview I at 13.

[215] Red Book, Chapter 7, ¶2.

[216] *Id.*

[217] Baron Interview.

[218] IG Report at 3.

[219] *Id.*

[220] *Id.*

[221] Smith Interview I at 14.

[222] Smith Interview II at 2 (citing Red Book, Chapter 2, part 1, at 2-5, no. 9a.).

staff to Berger following the October 2 document removal may have substantially compromised a proper law enforcement investigation and the recovery of all stolen documents. If Berger took other documents than those he was caught with or that he had admitted taking, a surprise search was more likely to recover them. In any event, the public would have more confidence that he did not take other documents.

C. Personnel Action

Following its investigation, the Archives IG determined that Archives staff erred in facilitating access to classified information in an unauthorized setting on five occasions.[223] Additionally, the Archives IG found fault with the manner in which Archives staff notified the appropriate authorities following the removal of classified information from the Archives.[224] The Information Security Manual requires Archives personnel to immediately notify the Department of Justice by the fastest means possible.[225]

The Archives IG identified a series of violations by five Archives employees. The Archives IG determined the provision of access to SCI and SAP materials in an unauthorized setting violated 18 U.S.C. § 793(f) relating to losing defense information, 18 U.S.C § 1924 (a) relating to the unauthorized removal and retention of classified documents or materials, Director of Central Intelligence Directive 6/9, Section 2.3.2 relating to Sensitive Compartment Information Facilities, and the agency's own Information Security Manual.[226] Once there was a suspicion that Berger may have removed classified information, first raised during the September 2 visit, Archives officials should have reported the incident immediately to a law enforcement entity.[227] Failure to do so was a violation of National Archives procedures.[228] Archives staff repeatedly failed to contact law enforcement when Berger's suspicious activity resurfaced during the October 2 visit.[229] Archives staff thwarted a proper investigation by law

---

[223] IG Report at 2.

[224] *Id.*

[225] *Id.* quoting Red Book.

[226] NARA OIG Briefing Paper, Samuel R. Berger, et al, 04-001-GC (Jan. 9, 2006) [hereinafter NARA OIG Briefing Paper].

[227] *Id.*

[228] Red Book, Chapter 1, Section 5.f.

[229] NARA OIG Briefing Paper.

enforcement by contacting Berger, the subject of a criminal investigation, several times by telephone.[230]

Following the receipt of the Archives IG Report, Allen Weistein, the current Archivist of the United States delegated the personnel inquiry to Henry Leibowitz, the agency's human resources director.[231] Leibowitz's inquiry examined the actions of four Archives employees – Smith, her supervisor Sharon Fawcett, Gary Stern, and Lewis Bellardo, the deputy Archivist.[232] Ultimately, Leibowitz issued three administrative sanctions, a "Counselling (sic) Letter" to Bellardo, and written "Reprimand Letters" to Stern and Smith.[233] All three employees appealed the sanctions to the Archivist.[234] On appeal, Bellardo's letter was withdrawn.[235] Sharon Fawcett received a letter stating that there was no grounds for discipline.[236] None of the Archives employees received a reduction in pay or any changes in their job titles or professional responsibilities.[237]

Gary Stern received a written Letter of Reprimand on June 27, 2006.[238] Such letters remain in the employee's official personnel file for two years. Leibowitz found Stern to have exercised a lack of judgment for failing to notify law enforcement officials in a timely manner.[239] Stern, however, was absolved by Leibowitz of violating any security procedures.[240] Leibowitz's decision was appealed to the Archivist, and on October 3, 2006, the personnel sanction was upheld.[241] On appeal, however, Stern did win the opportunity to have the Letter of Reprimand removed from his official personnel

---

[230] Smith Report at 6-7; IG Report at 12-13; NARA OIG Briefing Paper.

[231] Baron Interview.

[232] When the allegations of Berger's misconduct were brought to the attention of the Archivist, he delegated the agency's response and investigation to the deputy archivist, Lewis Bellardo.

[233] Baron Interview.

[234] *Id.*

[235] *Id.*

[236] *Id..*

[237] *Id.*

[238] *Id.*

[239] *Id.*

[240] *Id.*

[241] *Id.*

file.[242] The removal of the letter from the personnel file makes the sanction invisible to other potential government employers.[243] That said, Stern would, however, be required to disclose the sanction were he asked about it in the course of a job application or background check.[244]

Nancy Smith received a written Letter of Reprimand on June 27, 2006.[245] Leibowitz determined that Smith lacked judgment in leaving Berger alone in her office, and that the use of her office for the document review was not a good practice.[246] Smith appealed to the Archivist. In an October 3, 2006 letter, the Archivist affirmed that Smith had lacked judgment in leaving Berger alone in her office, but upon a determination by the security office that Smith did not intentionally violate any security directive, and that any security breach by using her office was only a technical violation, that ground for reprimand was removed.[247] Like Stern, however, Smith's letter was removed from her official personnel file.[248]

D. Archives Substantially Revises Procedures

On March 31, 2004, Deputy Archivist and Chief of Staff of the National Archives Lewis J. Bellardo issued comprehensive new guidelines for the handling of classified materials.[249] The new guidelines were transmitted agency-wide in the form of a six page Interim Guidance memorandum entitled, "Access to Materials Containing Classified Information in NARA Research Rooms by Non-Governmental Persons."[250] The comprehensive new guidance specifically addresses many of the lax procedures in force during Berger's visits.

---

[242] Id.

[243] Id.

[244] Id.

[245] Id.

[246] Id.

[247] Id.

[248] Id.

[249] Lewis J. Bellardo, Deputy Archivist of the United States and Chief of Staff to the National Archives and Records Administration (NARAA), Interim Guidance 1600-5, Access to Materials Containing Classified Information in NARA Research Rooms by Non-Governmental Persons, March 31, 2004 [hereinafter Interim Guidance].

[250] Id.

Under the new guidelines, classified materials must be reviewed in a dedicated room, not an active office.[251] The dedicated room must be free of all non-authorized materials.[252] Under the new rules, Berger would not be permitted to review documents in Nancy Smith's personal office. Likewise, Berger would not be permitted to review documents in an office setting that contains other classified materials which Berger was not cleared to see.

The guidelines call for all notes to be taken on paper easily identified as that provided by the National Archives.[253] Classified materials are now to be handed to researchers one box at a time, and only one box may be on the researchers table at any one time.[254] Cell phones and other electronic equipment are no longer permitted in research rooms.[255] The new guidelines call for the implementation of closed circuit television monitoring and recording equipment so that the classified materials can be further protected.[256] The closed circuit television equipment is to serve as "a deterrent measure and aids in any investigations."[257]

The guidelines offer specific guidance for classified production reviews pursuant to subpoena, whether this be under the authority of a congressional committee, independent investigation or commission, or by a court.[258] Important new aspects include:

- Researchers are to be continuously monitored by Archives staff.
- Continuous monitoring means the Archives staff must be watching the researcher full time, and not while performing other duties.
- Provide researchers with numbered copies of the documents.
- Maintain a second control set of documents and document inventory log.
- Each researcher is required to sign a receipt as each box is provided for review.

---

[251] Interim Guidance at ¶ 4(b).

[252] *Id.* at ¶ 4(d).

[253] *Id.* at ¶ 6(a).

[254] *Id.* at ¶ 6(d).

[255] *Id.* at ¶ 6(b).

[256] *Id.* at ¶ 6(c).

[257] *Id.*

[258] *Id.* at ¶ 8.

- On return, the Archives staff are to examine each box before the researcher is permitted to leave the research room.
- If the researcher believes he/she requires the original documents, and not copies, a written waiver request must be processed through the offices of the agency's General Counsel and head of Security.[259]

This comprehensive new guidance specifically addresses many of the lax procedures in force prior to April 2004 and should ameliorate the need for a further overhaul of the security procedures for the review of classified materials.

VI. Effects on 9/11 Commission's Work – Not Knowable Whether All Documents Were Produced

A. Inspector General and Justice Department Clash Over Notifying 9/11 Commission

FINDING: *The Archives Inspector General and Justice Department officials clashed over notifying the 9/11 Commission of the extent of Berger's document removal and the fact that Berger had access to original documents that may have been responsive to Commission document requests. No one told the 9/11 Commission that Berger had access to original documents.*

In January 2004, Archives Inspector General Paul Brachfeld contemplated whether Archives officials or officials from his office had a responsibility to notify the 9/11 Commission about the Berger matter.[260] Brachfeld was concerned that during the course of a criminal investigation being conducted by the Department of Justice, officials at Justice might be reluctant to notify the 9/11 Commission.[261] Brachfeld recognized that prosecutors are rightfully tightlipped about pending investigations, but believed that disclosure of Berger's actions was necessary to allow the 9/11 Commission the ability to evaluate Berger's credibility and truthfulness as a witness.[262] Berger had access to original documents during three of his four visits to the Archives, and consequently could have removed documents that were responsive to 9/11 EOP requests. Brachfeld also was concerned that the 9/11 Commission might not have been fully aware of the scope of

---

[259] *Id.* at ¶¶ 9-10.

[260] Interview by Gov't Reform Comm. Staff with Paul Brachfeld, Inspector Gen., NARA, and Kelly Maltagliati, Special Agent, NARA, in Wash., D.C. (Dec. 1, 2006) [hereinafter Brachfeld and Maltagliati Interview, Dec. 1, 2006].

[261] Brachfeld and Maltagliati Interview, Dec. 1, 2006.

[262] *Id.*

Berger's alleged misdeeds.[263]   Brachfeld said there was reasonable evidence Berger might be obstructing the 9/11 Commission's investigation and the 9/11 Commission ought to know that.[264]

On January 14, 2004, Brachfeld met with Howard Sklamberg, one of the trial attorneys at the Justice Department handling the Berger matter for the Public Integrity Section.[265]   Brachfeld wanted answers to three questions: had the Justice Department notified the 9/11 Commission of Berger's actions; had the Justice Department identified the extent of potential damage to the Commission's document requests; that is, had the Department fully accounted for all documents Berger may have removed; and had the Department communicated the possible extent of the damage to the 9/11 Commission.[266]

That same day, the 9/11 Commission conducted its private interview with Sandy Berger.[267]   Whether Brachfeld or the Justice Department knew that Berger was being questioned by the Commission is not known. Berger's public testimony occurred on March 24, 2004.[268]

On March 22, 2004, two days before Berger's public testimony, Brachfeld received a telephone call from two Justice Department officials, Chief of the Counterespionage Section John Dion and Deputy Assistant Attorney General for the Criminal Division Bruce Swartz.[269]

The purpose of the call was twofold. First, the Justice Department officials wanted to thank Brachfeld for suspending his internal inquiry while the Justice Department pursued its criminal matter against Berger. Second, the Justice Department wanted to notify Brachfeld that Berger was to testify before the 9/11 Commission. Brachfeld was advised that the Justice Department was not going to notify the 9/11 Commission about the pending criminal investigation of Berger.[270]

---

[263] *Id.*

[264] *Id.*

[265] *Id.*

[266] *Id.*

[267] The 9/11 Report, see notes at 479-509.

[268] The 9/11 Comm'n (March 24, 2004) (testimony of Samuel L. (sic) Berger); http://www.911commission.gov/hearings/hearing8/berger_statement.pdf (last visited Dec. 17, 2006).

[269] Brachfeld and Maltagliati Interview, Dec. 1, 2006.

[270] *Id.*

This took Brachfeld by surprise as he was unaware that the 9/11 Commission was scheduled to take Berger's public testimony.[271] According to Brachfeld, they stated that Brachfeld ultimately may be at risk for not notifying the 9/11 Commission of the circumstances involving Berger's visits to the National Archives.[272] Brachfeld was also advised that the Justice Department believed that notifying the 9/11 Commission about the Berger incident could compromise their investigation.[273]

Dion's recollection of this call is not clear.[274] Dion recalls speaking with Brachfeld on numerous occasions, both in person and on the telephone.[275] Dion said it was possible that he and Brachfeld conversed about the differing obligations of the Inspector General's Office and the Department of Justice about notifying the 9/11 Commission.[276] In Dion's view, the Justice Department's first obligation was to conduct its criminal investigation in the proper way.[277]

Brachfeld told Committee staff he found himself in an extremely precarious position.[278] He was concerned that Berger's public testimony was scheduled to go forward before the 9/11 Commission without the Commission knowing that its witness might not be reliable and trustworthy.[279] On the one hand, he felt obligated to notify the 9/11 Commission that one of their witnesses' veracity and credibility may be in question, but on the other hand, he felt obligated not to divulge this information as it may affect a pending criminal investigation by the Justice Department.[280] On several occasions Brachfeld referred to Dion as a powerful and influential Justice Department official, and consequently Brachfeld believed it was career suicide to cross Dion.[281]

---

[271] *Id.*

[272] *Id.*

[273] Brachfeld and Maltagliati Interview, Dec. 1, 2006.

[274] Telephonic Interview by Gov't Reform Comm. Staff with John Dion, Chief of the Counterespionage Section, DOJ, in Wash., D.C. (Jan. 8, 2007) [hereinafter Dion Telephonic Interview].

[275] Dion Telephonic Interview.

[276] *Id..*

[277] *Id..*

[278] *Id.*

[279] *Id.*

[280] *Id.*

[281] *Id.*

To protect himself, on the March 22 call, Brachfeld requested an inoculation letter from Swartz to insulate himself from charges that he willfully failed to notify the 9/11 Commission about facts relevant to the Berger matter.[282] According to Brachfeld, Swartz agreed to provide such a letter.[283] When asked about the inoculation letter, Dion "did not specifically recall" discussing such a letter with Brachfeld, but said that did not mean it was not discussed.[284] The Justice Department never provided this letter.[285]

On March 25 or 26, 2004, Brachfeld called Thomas Reilly at the Justice Department.[286] Reilly and Sklamberg were the trial attorneys handling the Berger matter.[287] Reilly worked for Dion in the Counterespionage Section, and Sklamberg worked for Noel Hillman in the Public Integrity Section.[288] The purpose of this call was to discuss with Justice specific witnesses the Archives IG's office was permitted to interview. Up until this point, the IG's internal inquiry had been stalled pending further notice from the Department of Justice about the progression of the Berger investigation.[289] According to Brachfeld, Reilly agreed to confer with other Justice Department officials and follow up with Brachfeld with the names of specific witnesses that the Archives IG's office could proceed with interviewing.[290]

Brachfeld was concerned that the longer his internal investigation remained on hold, the less productive it would be considering that witnesses' memories tend to fade over time. Despite Reilly's commitment to provide such a list, Brachfeld never received it.[291] On this call, Brachfeld expressed his concern to Reilly that the 9/11 Commission had not been notified about the Berger matter.[292]

---

[282] *Id.*

[283] *Id.*

[284] Dion Telephonic Interview.

[285] Brachfeld and Maltagliati Interview, Dec. 1, 2006.

[286] *Id.*

[287] *Id.*

[288] *Id.*; Berger, Factual Basis for Plea at 3.

[289] Brachfeld and Maltagliati Interview, Dec. 1, 2006.

[290] *Id.*

[291] *Id.*

[292] *Id.*

Frustrated, on April 6, 2004, Brachfeld called Glenn Fine, the Inspector General for the Justice Department.[293] Brachfeld related his two concerns to Fine – whether the 9/11 Commission was properly notified and whether the document production was tainted by the fact Berger may have removed original documents.[294] According to Brachfeld, Fine agreed to look into the matter.[295]

Fine organized a meeting for April 9, 2004.[296] Present at the meeting, according to Brachfeld, were Assistant Attorney General for the Criminal Division Christopher Wray; Wray's Chief of Staff John Richter; Dion; Swartz; Sklamberg; Reilly; Fine; and Brachfeld's principle investigator.[297] According to Brachfeld, the purpose of the meeting was to discuss whether the Justice Department had an obligation to disclose facts relating to the Berger matter to the 9/11 Commission.[298] In Brachfeld's view, Berger knowingly removed documents and therefore, may have purposely impeded the 9/11 investigation.[299] Brachfeld felt that Christopher Wray was sympathetic to the dilemma.[300] Brachfeld told the group that pertinent original documents might have been removed by Berger.[301]

A debate emerged between Brachfeld and Bruce Swartz about whether the 9/11 Commission received all documents.[302] Brachfeld thought the Justice Department was focusing exclusively on the September 2 and October 2 visits by Berger, and by not examining Berger's first two visits, they were failing to consider important evidence.[303] Swartz remained fixated on his conclusion that Berger took nothing else, and the 9/11

---

[293] *Id.*

[294] *Id.*

[295] *Id.*

[296] *Id.*

[297] *Id.*; Interview by Gov't Reform Comm. Staff with Glenn Fine, Inspector Gen., U.S. Dep't of Justice [hereinafter DOJ], in Wash., D.C. (Dec. 7, 2006) [hereinafter Fine Interview]. Fine confirmed the personnel assembled for the meeting, with the exception of Sklamberg and Reilly.

[298] Brachfeld and Maltagliati Interview, Dec. 1, 2006.

[299] *Id.*

[300] *Id.*

[301] *Id.*

[302] *Id.*

[303] *Id.*

Commission received a complete production.[304] Swartz insisted that Berger was examining only copies of documents, and therefore the damage to the 9/11 Commission was limited.[305]

Swartz and the other Justice Department officials failed to grasp, in Brachfeld's view, that Berger had access to a large number of original and unique documents on his first two visits to the Archives on May 30, 2002 and July 18, 2003.[306] Brachfeld reiterated his point by referring to Smith's statement "six months ago" where she said, "she would never know what if any original documents were missing."[307] Disagreeing, Swartz responded that Smith said she was present at all times.[308] Brachfeld countered that Smith was working at her desk and Berger was at a conference table, that Berger had an overcoat with him, and there was no way for Smith to have seen everything.[309] According to Brachfeld, Wray and Fine indicated they understood Brachfeld's concerns, and both Wray and Fine asked whether the FBI had questioned relevant witnesses regarding the first two visits.[310] The FBI stated that they did not question Berger about the first two visits.[311] With confirmation of this, Wray and Fine agreed with Brachfeld that they could not be certain the 9/11 Commission received all responsive documents.[312]

The schism between Brachfeld and Swartz on the issue of the completeness of the 9/11 Commission document production never abated.[313] As the meeting concluded, Christopher Wray gave Brachfeld his assurance that the 9/11 Commission was to be notified.[314] Fine's recollection was Wray agreed Daniel Levin, the Justice Department's

---

[304] Id.

[305] Id.

[306] Id.

[307] Id.; See also, Smith Interview I at 12. ("Ms. Smith advised that Mr. Berger was served originals on his July 18, 2003 visit. She would never know what if any original documents were missing. There was no absolute way to verify if any originals were removed.")

[308] Brachfeld and Maltagliati Interview, Dec. 1, 2006.

[309] Id.

[310] Id.

[311] Id.

[312] Id.

[313] Id.

[314] Id.

liaison to the 9/11 Commission, was to communicate this information to the 9/11 Commission General Counsel Daniel Marcus.[315]

The information communicated by the Justice Department to the 9/11 Commission never was specifically outlined to Brachfeld.[316] On multiple occasions throughout April and May, 2004, Brachfeld attempted to follow up with the Justice Department to see if it followed through with its commitment to notify the 9/11 Commission.[317] Not until May 26, did word make its way through Glenn Fine to Brachfeld that "relevant information" had been given to the 9/11 Commission.[318] Concerned what "relevant information" meant in the eyes of Justice Department officials, Brachfeld attempted numerous times to follow up with Justice.[319]

On July 19, 2004, the Associated Press first reported that Berger was the subject of a criminal investigation for removing highly classified documents from the National Archives.[320] This occurred just days before the July 22, 2004 release of the Commission's Final Report.[321]

Brachfeld's level of concern continued into the fall of 2004.[322] In November, Brachfeld discussed with Fine the prospect of having a follow up meeting with the relevant Justice Department officials.[323]

On November 5, a meeting was convened with Justice officials, Dion, Swartz, and Hillman.[324] At this meeting, Dion and Swartz told Brachfeld the 9/11 Commission was not informed that Berger had access to original documents.[325] On hearing this, Noel

---

[315] Fine Interview.

[316] Brachfeld and Maltagliati Interview, Dec. 1, 2006.

[317] *Id.*

[318] *Id.*

[319] *Id.*

[320] Solomon July 19, 2004 article.

[321] The 9/11 Comm'n website, http://www.9-11commission.gov/ (last visited Dec. 17, 2006).

[322] Brachfeld and Maltagliati Interview, Dec. 1, 2006.

[323] *Id.*

[324] *Id.*

[325] *Id.*

Hillman appeared angry and perturbed, according to Brachfeld.[326] Brachfeld said he noticed Swartz becoming visibly agitated as Hillman's dissatisfaction became evident.[327] Although Brachfeld had long suspected a substantial exposure in the 9/11 Commission's investigation, it was not until this meeting that he realized his worst fears were true.[328] When questioned about this meeting, Dion recalled being in attendance, but did not have a "specific recollection" of what occurred at this meeting.[329]

During the November 5 meeting, Brachfeld revisited Swartz's March 22 offer to provide an inoculation letter.[330] In Brachfeld's view, such a letter would provide some measure of protection to Brachfeld from any later-alleged wrongdoing associated with not notifying the 9/11 Commission of the facts of the Berger matter.[331] During this meeting, however, Swartz was noncommittal about such a letter, telling Brachfeld that he would have to check his notes from March 22, and Swartz believed any such letter would be applicable only to the 9/11 Commission and not Congressional oversight committees.[332]

On November 19, 2004, Archives IG investigators met with the FBI to discuss their investigation.[333] During this meeting, the FBI confirmed to Archives IG investigators, that they did not question Berger about his first two visits to the Archives.[334] The Archives IG's staff asked the FBI case agents why. The FBI told Brachfeld's staff that they did not question Berger about his first two visits because the first visit on May 30, 2002 was not relevant to the 9/11 Commission document requests and during the second visit on July 18, 2003, Berger was supervised for the duration of his visit by Nancy Smith.[335]

---

[326] *Id.*

[327] *Id.*

[328] *Id.*

[329] Dion Telephonic Interview.

[330] Brachfeld and Maltagliati Interview, Dec. 1, 2006.

[331] *Id.*

[332] *Id.*

[333] *Id.*

[334] *Id.*

[335] *Id.*

On November 23, 2004, a follow up meeting at the Justice Department occurred.[336] In attendance, according to Brachfeld were Dion, Swartz, Hillman, Reilly, and the FBI case agents.[337] Brachfeld raised the question of why the 9/11 Commission was not told that Berger had access to originals.[338] Brachfeld asked Reilly whether the Justice Department would be willing to go back and look more carefully at this question.[339] According to Brachfeld, Reilly said no, indicating "it would take a long time" and much effort.[340] Brachfeld continued to press his case that the opportunity existed for Berger to remove crucial documents.[341] Hillman was shown a copy of the John Laster e-mail where he alerted Smith about seeing Berger with documents folded and stuffed in his socks on his third visit when he had access to original documents.[342] After the Laster e-mail was read, Brachfeld asked every person in the room to pull up their suit pants and look at their dress socks.[343] He asked everyone to consider whether "something white" might be easily noticed if papers were lodged in their socks.[344] Brachfeld pressed Justice Department officials about why they did not consider John Laster and his contemporaneous e-mail more indicative of Berger's culpability.[345]

Brachfeld asked whether the Justice Department had obtained Berger's medical records to see if he was suffering from phlebitis or other medical condition that might cause him to need to wear a white sleeve on his leg.[346] The Justice Department acknowledged that they did not look into Berger's medical history.[347] At this point,

---

[336] *Id.*

[337] *Id.*

[338] *Id.*

[339] *Id.*

[340] *Id.*

[341] *Id.*

[342] *Id.*

[343] *Id.*

[344] *Id.*

[345] *Id.*

[346] *Id.*

[347] *Id.*

according to Brachfeld, Swartz became agitated, and screamed, "Are you accusing me of failing to tell the 9/11 Commission?"[348]

After that meeting, Brachfeld conferred separately with Hillman. Hillman acknowledged if Justice had known all the details earlier – that Berger had access to originals – the Department would have told the 9/11 Commission more.[349] Brachfeld protested that he had been communicating this point to the Justice Department – at least since April.[350] Hillman agreed to interview Smith personally.[351]

According to Brachfeld and his staff, Hillman personally interviewed Smith on December 10, 2004.[352] Present at this interview was the Archives IG's lead investigator, Special Agent Kelly Maltagliati.[353] Maltagliati told Committee staff that at the conclusion of Hillman's questioning of Smith, she witnessed Hillman instruct the FBI case agents present that they were to go back and look at documents from all of Berger's visits.[354] To the Archives IG's knowledge, the FBI never reviewed the documents from Berger's first two visits.[355]

On April 1, 2005, the Justice Department announced its plea agreement with Berger. In speaking to the press, Hillman startled Brachfeld by stating the Justice Department's investigation found no evidence of Berger trying to hide anything from the 9/11 Commission, and the Commission had access to all documents it requested.[356]

On April 13, 2005, Brachfeld met with Hillman to discuss these points. According to Brachfeld, Hillman now believed that Berger was being honest with the Justice Department and the risk that he took additional documents was minimal.[357]

---

[348] *Id.* When questioned about this meeting, Dion recalled being in attendance, but did not have a "specific recollection" of what occurred at this meeting. Dion Telephonic Interview.

[349] Brachfeld and Maltagliati Interview, Dec. 1, 2006.

[350] *Id.*

[351] *Id.*

[352] *Id.*

[353] *Id.*

[354] *Id.*

[355] *Id.*

[356] *Id.*

[357] *Id.*

Hillman explained to Brachfeld that his public statements were narrowly tailored to the facts included in the plea agreement, and Hillman could only confirm that the 9/11 Commission received all documents relating to the Millennium Alert After Action Review.[358]

Despite all of these considerations, according to the Archives IG and his staff, the FBI or the Department of Justice never questioned Berger about his May 30, 2002 and July 18, 2003 visits.[359] Berger had access to a large volume of original documents on these two visits. On May 30, 2002, Berger was provided several boxes of original and unique documents, including the original, uncopied Staff Member Office Files of Richard Clarke and original, uncopied, unique NSC numbered documents.[360] During Berger's second visit on July 18, 2003, he was provided original, and uncopied Staff Member Office Files and original, and uncopied NSC numbered documents.

B. Justice Department Convinced Berger's Document Theft Limited to What He Admitted

FINDING: *There is no basis for concluding Berger did not remove original documents responsive to 9/11 Commission requests during the May 30, 2002 and July 18, 2003 visits to the National Archives. Nevertheless, the Justice Department's representations to the 9/11 Commission left the impression that Berger's document theft was limited to what he admitted to taking.*

On November 13, 2006, Committee staff interviewed John Dion and Bruce Swartz of the Justice Department. Swartz explained that a primary focus of their investigation was whether the 9/11 Commission was deprived of any documents.[361] They concluded that it had not.[362]

According to Swartz, after conducting interviews with staff from the National Archives, and after having the FBI conduct a review of the document files that Berger examined with the assistance of Archives officials, the Justice Department concluded that there was no evidence of Berger taking any additional documents.[363] The Justice

---

[358] *Id.*

[359] *Id.*

[360] Smith Report at 2; PMS Interview at 3.

[361] Interview by Gov't Reform Comm. Staff with John Dion, Chief of the Counterespionage Section, DOJ, and Bruce Swartz, Deputy Assistant Attorney Gen., DOJ, in Wash., D.C. (Nov. 13, 2006) [hereinafter Dion and Swartz Interview].

[362] Dion and Swartz Interview.

[363] *Id..*

Department concluded that Berger took the documents for personal convenience.[364] The Justice Department was comforted by the fact that Berger was examining printed copies of e-mails and the documents that Berger admitted to taking were all different versions of the same after-action report.[365] The Justice Department apparently would have been more concerned if Berger took different documents instead of different versions of the same document.[366] Swartz said the Department concluded the after-action "documents he took were, in all probability, the only documents he took."[367] Dion told Committee staff that the after-action reports he took all existed elsewhere, and he was merely looking at copies, not originals.[368] Moreover, according to Dion, the after-action report documents were beneficial to the Clinton administration – the documents portrayed the White House as being engaged on the subject of terrorism.[369] Had the documents been damaging to Berger or the Clinton administration, Dion stated that the Department might have taken a different approach.[370]

When asked by Committee staff how they could be so sure Berger did not take original documents during his first two visits, Dion and Swartz explained that it was difficult to prove a negative.[371] They stated that the Justice Department could not prove that he did not take anything else, but found no evidence that suggested he did.[372] Dion and Swartz also stated that Berger established further credibility in his proffer by disclosing the embarrassing manner in which he stole the documents by stashing them in a construction site.[373] Committee staff asked Dion and Swartz whether they ever polygraphed Berger pursuant to paragraph 11(c) of Berger's Plea Agreement which requires Berger to "voluntarily submit to polygraph examination."[374] They said they did not.

---

[364] *Id.*.

[365] *Id.*.

[366] *Id.*.

[367] *Id.*.

[368] *Id.*.

[369] *Id.*.

[370] *Id.*.

[371] *Id.*.

[372] *Id.*.

[373] *Id.*.

[374] Plea Agreement at ¶3(c).

The lack of interest in Berger's first two visits is disturbing. The May 30, 2002 document review was on the same subject matter as Berger's other three visits. Berger spent May 30, 2002 looking at Richard Clarke's original office files.[375] Had Berger seen a "smoking gun" or other document he did not want to be brought to an investigatory panel's attention, he could have removed it on this visit. The May 2002 research session by Berger was sufficiently critical to the 9/11 Commission's document requests that on receipt of the official EOP requests, the Archives staff's first action was to pull the materials that had been set aside for Berger's prior visit in May 2002.[376]

The 9/11 Commission reported that at least one memo written by Clarke contained Berger's handwritten notations. On December 4, 1999, Clarke advised Berger to attack al Qaeda facilities in the week before January 1, 2000. According to the 9/11 Commission, in the margin adjacent to this suggestion, Berger rejected Clarke's suggestion to hit al Qaeda and wrote "no."[377]

The lack of interest in Berger's second visit, July 18, 2003, is inexplicable. The FBI told the Archives IG's staff that no exposure existed because Berger was under constant supervision by Smith.[378] This is troubling in light of Smith's statements that "she would never know what if any original documents were missing."[379] According to Berger himself, Smith spent time "working at her desk" while he reviewed materials on July 18, 2003.[380] Berger also said that on July 18, 2003 he received a "half dozen" phone calls where he was left alone in Smith's office.[381] Berger admits to removing classified documents – his handwritten notes – on July 18, 2003. The Archives IG's memorandum following Berger's interview stated as follows:

> At the end of the day, Berger tri-folded his notes and put them in his suit pocket. He took the opportunity to do this when Ms. Smith was out of her office due to him being on a private phone call.

The Justice Department was unacceptably incurious about Berger's Archives visits on May 30, 2002 and July 18, 2003. The Justice Department never notified the 9/11 Commission that Berger viewed a large number of original documents on these first

---

[375] PMS Interview at 3.

[376] PMS Interview at 4.

[377] The 9/11 Report , Chapter 6, n. 11.

[378] Brachfeld and Maltagliati Interview, Dec. 1, 2006.

[379] Smith Interview I at 12.

[380] Berger Interview at 3.

[381] Berger Interview at 3.

two visits. The Justice Department failed to subpoena Berger's medical records to determine if there was any medical reason for him to have white-colored material on his lower leg. The Justice Department failed to administer a polygraph examination.

The Justice Department failed to explain to the 9/11 Commission all the relevant facts about all of Berger's visits, especially his first two visits where he had access to a large collection of original documents. There is no basis for concluding that Berger did not remove original documents during his first two visits to the National Archives. It is not knowable whether Berger removed critical documents responsive to the 9/11 Commission during these first two visits. Given Berger's admission that he removed his classified notes during the July 18, 2003 visit, he certainly could have removed other classified documents. The Justice Department's statement that Berger's statements are credible after being caught is misplaced. One would not rely on the fox to be truthful after being nabbed in a hen house. The Justice Department apparently did.

C. Hillman's Public Statements Are Incomplete and Misleading; 9/11 Commission May Have Been Deprived of Original Documents

FINDING: *The public statements of the former chief of the Justice Department's Public Integrity Section, Noel Hillman were incomplete and misleading. Because Berger had access to original documents on May 30, 2002, and July 18, 2003, there is no basis for his statement that "nothing was lost to the public or the process."*

While the Justice Department's investigation focused on the September 2 and October 2 visits by Berger, and Berger's plea was based on documents he removed on these two visits, Department officials took the unusual step of publicly confirming their *belief* – which cannot be proven – that the 9/11 Commission received all the documents they requested.

A Justice Department press release about Berger's guilty plea stated "[o]n September 2, 2003, and again on October 2, Berger concealed and removed a total of five copies of classified documents from the Archives. The documents were different versions of a single document."[382] Speaking to the press at the time of Berger's plea, Noel Hillman, chief of the Department's Public Integrity Section stated, Berger "'did not have an intent to hide any of the content of the documents' or conceal facts from the

---

[382] Press Release, DOJ, Former Nat'l Sec. Advisor Samuel Berger Pleads Guilty to Knowingly Removing Classified Info. from the Nat'l Archives (Apr. 1, 2005) (on file with Gov't Reform Comm.).

commission investigating the Sept. 11, 2001, attacks."[383] On April 2, 2005, *The New York Times* wrote:

> The department's investigation had found no evidence that Mr. Berger had intended to hide anything from the Sept. 11 commission. Indeed, the commission had access to all the original reports on the 2000 assessment.[384]

Along similar lines, *The Washington Post* reported, "Hillman noted that Berger only had copies of the documents – not the originals – and so was not charged with the more serious crime of destroying documents."[385] Hillman also stated, "Nothing was lost to the public or the process."[386]

Hillman's comments were incomplete and misleading. The Department's investigation and Berger's plea agreement were limited in scope to the documents he admittedly removed on September 2 and October 2. Berger, however, had access to original materials on two other visits to the Archives, on May 30, 2002 and on July 18, 2003.[387] While the Justice Department had convinced itself that Berger had not taken any documents beyond what he admitted to, and although they asserted that they had found no evidence to suggest otherwise, it is impossible to know whether this is true.

Hillman knew that Justice Department officials had not told the 9/11 Commission that Berger had had access to original documents. He attended at least two meetings with officials from the Archives IG's office, the purpose of which was to discuss obligations to the 9/11 Commission. Archives IG officials were steadfast in their belief that the Justice Department had an obligation to notify the 9/11 Commission of all relevant facts, notably that Berger spent two days at the Archives reviewing large quantities of original, uncopied, unique documents. Hillman was present on November 5, 2004 when John Dion and Bruce Swartz confirmed to Brachfeld that the 9/11 Commission never was told Berger had access to originals. Hillman was present on November 23, 2004 when John Laster's e-mail to Smith was read. Laster, one of four Archives staff members with a security clearance high enough to handle these classified documents – a security clearance higher than that of Berger's own former deputy National Security Advisor –

---

[383] Carol D. Leonnig, Berger Is Likely to Face Fine, WASH. POST, Apr. 2, 2005, at A8 [hereinafter Leonnig Apr. 2, 2005 article].

[384] Eric Lichtblau, *Clinton Aide Pleads Guilty to Taking Secret Papers*, N.Y. TIMES, Apr. 2, 2005, at A10.

[385] Leonnig Apr. 2, 2005 article.

[386] Johanna Neuman, *Top Clinton Aide Admits he Pilfered Documents*, LA TIMES, April 2, 2005, at A1.

[387] IG Report at 5.

notified Smith that he saw what he thought were white papers lodged in Berger's socks. Hillman, himself, conducted an interview of Smith. In September 2004, Smith had stated "she would never know what if any original documents were missing."[388] Nevertheless, Hillman's public statements did not account for these facts.

Committee staff called Hillman, now a United States District Judge in Camden, New Jersey. Hillman declined to make himself available for an interview.

D. 9/11 Commission Relies on Assurances by the Justice Department

FINDING: *The 9/11 Commission relied on assurances from the Department of Justice that a full and complete production was made, and that no original or any other responsive documents were withheld. No one told the 9/11 Commission that Berger had access to original documents. The 9/11 Commission was specifically interested in the office files of White House terrorism advisor Richard Clarke, and never was told that Berger had access to Clarke's original office files on May 30, 2002, and July 18, 2003.*

Access to White House documents was a critical component of the 9/11 Commission's investigation.[389] The Commission was interested in understanding the terrorism-related considerations at the White House before September 11, 2001.[390] Under agreements reached with the incumbent White House, the Commission was to obtain all relevant staff-level documents, up to but not including, documents prepared for the President.[391] These were considered protected by executive privilege.[392] The incumbent White House was concerned that any concession it made to the 9/11 Commission would establish precedent.[393]

---

[388] Brachfeld and Maltagliati Interview, Dec. 1, 2006; See also, Smith Interview I at 12. ("Ms. Smith advised that Mr. Berger was served originals on his July 18, 2003 visit. She would never know what if any original documents were missing. There was no absolute way to verify if any originals were removed."

[389] Interview by Gov't Reform Comm. Staff with Dan Marcus, Gen. Counsel, The 9/11 Comm'n, in Wash., D.C. (Dec. 8, 2006) [hereinafter Marcus Interview].

[390] Marcus Interview.

[391] *Id.*.

[392] *Id.*.

[393] *Id.*.

According to Philip Zelikow, the Executive Director of the 9/11 Commission, the Commissioners and staff conducted a "lengthy and detailed private interrogation with Mr. Berger."[394] This interview took place on January 14, 2004.[395] The Commission took public testimony from Berger on March 24, 2004.[396]

One area of particular interest to the 9/11 Commission was the papers of terrorism adviser Richard Clarke.[397] According to 9/11 Commission General Counsel Daniel Marcus, Clarke was a prolific writer of reports and e-mails.[398] Clarke generated a huge volume of written material.[399] The Commission was interested in seeing Clarke's files.[400] We were "very interested in draft reports with handwritten notes," Marcus explained.[401]

According to Marcus, the Commission staff believed Berger never changed anything in Clarke's memos and papers, he just passed them on up the line.[402] The mechanics of the agreement the Commission had with the White House allowed for production of all documents unless the White House could demonstrate affirmatively it was actually shown to the President.[403] The Commission staff believed they were able to see many documents that were likely shown to the President, as long as there was no overt evidence to prove that the President actually looked at the papers.[404]

9/11 Commission Co-Chairs Tom Kean and Lee Hamilton became aware Berger was under investigation by the Justice Department in early 2004. In their book, they describe the following:

---

[394] Telephonic Interview by Gov't Reform Comm. Staff with Philip Zelikow, Exec. Dir., The 9/11 Comm'n, in Wash., D.C. (Jan. 8, 2007) [hereinafter Zelikow Interview].

[395] The 9/11 Report, see notes at 479-509.

[396] The 9/11 Comm'n (March 24, 2004) (testimony of Samuel L. (sic) Berger); http://www.911commission.gov/hearings/hearing8/berger_statement.pdf (last visited Dec. 17, 2006).

[397] Marcus Interview.

[398] *Id.*.

[399] *Id.*.

[400] *Id.*.

[401] *Id.*.

[402] *Id.*.

[403] *Id.*.

[404] *Id.*.

Judge Gonzales [then White House Counsel] called both of us with strange news: Sandy Berger was under investigation by the Justice Department for taking highly classified documents . . . . The documents in question included an after-action report prepared by Richard Clarke that assessed the Clinton administration's response to terrorist threats accompanying the millennium celebrations.[405]

Marcus confirmed this account, and explained that Lee Hamilton advised Zelikow and him of what Gonzales had reported.[406] As Zelikow remembers, they were not aware of the Berger investigation at the time of Berger's private interview on January 14, 2004, but learned of it sometime before his public testimony.[407] Zelikow wished the Commission had known earlier.[408] While they would not have confronted Berger about the allegations, Zelikow said "they could have reflected on it" and it could have affected the credibility of Berger's answers.[409]

Marcus was separately advised of the Berger matter by Dion. As Marcus recalls, Dion was the designated official within the Justice Department to discuss the Berger matter with the 9/11 Commission staff.[410] Marcus told Committee staff that shortly after Hamilton told them Berger was the subject of a Justice Department investigation, he received a call from Dion.[411] Dion remembers this differently. As Dion recalls, the first communication to the 9/11 Commission staff was through Daniel Levin, the Justice Department's liaison to the 9/11 Commission.[412] As Dion recalls, the first he spoke with Marcus was at a meeting in Dion's office at the Justice Department.[413] The date of the meeting, according to Justice Department Criminal Division officials was April 16, 2004.[414] Dion does not specifically recall the date of the meeting, but said it may have

---

[405] Kean & Hamilton at 183.

[406] Marcus Interview.

[407] Zelikow Interview.

[408] *Id.*.

[409] *Id.*.

[410] Marcus Interview.

[411] *Id.*.

[412] Dion Telephonic Interview.

[413] *Id.*.

[414] *Id.*.

occurred before Berger's public testimony on March 24, 2004.[415] According to Marcus, he told Dion the 9/11 Commission was concerned that they may not have gotten all required documents.[416] Dion told Marcus the Department was planning to look into it.[417]

At some point, and Marcus cannot recall specifically when, Dion called and reported that the Department was assured the 9/11 Commission had received everything it requested.[418] Dion explained to Marcus that Berger had taken several versions of the same document.[419]

Dion did not tell Marcus enough. In his discussions with Dion, Marcus observed it was Dion's practice to confer as little information as possible.[420] According to Marcus, "Dion is not an expansive guy when talking about pending investigations."[421] With that said, Marcus did state that he "was led to believe Berger was not shown any unique documents."[422] Marcus believed Berger had been given copies of documents, or if originals, he thought the Archives had a copy, so he did not think Berger saw anything "unique."[423] Marcus was confident they received all responsive documents because that is what the Justice Department told him. The Justice Department did not tell Marcus that Berger had access to originals.[424] When explained by Committee staff that Berger had access to original documents on three visits to the Archives, Marcus was surprised, and acknowledged that he did not know that.[425] Marcus said if they had been told he had access to original documents, it would have raised concerns.[426]

---

[415] *Id.*.

[416] Marcus Interview.

[417] *Id.*.

[418] *Id.*.

[419] *Id.*.

[420] *Id.*.

[421] Marcus Interview.

[422] *Id.*.

[423] *Id.*.

[424] *Id.*.

[425] Marcus Interview.

[426] Marcus Interview.

According to Dion, he never discussed with 9/11 Commission officials whether Berger had access to original documents.[427] Dion told Commission officials that their investigation showed no reason to believe that the 9/11 Commission did not get all the information they sought.[428] Committee staff asked Dion how the Justice Department could be so assured that no other original documents were removed by Berger, and Dion responded that it was "a fair inference" to draw from the type of investigation that was being conducted.[429] Dion, "does not specifically recall" how extensively Berger was questioned about stealing other documents.[430] Committee staff asked whether Berger was questioned about the first two visits, and Dion replied, "I expect that he was, but do not have a specific recollection."[431]

Zelikow told Committee staff that the 9/11 Commission staff was highly concerned about the completeness and integrity of the document production from the White House.[432] Zelikow said that whenever a concern was raised that the Commission had not received a complete production in response to its document requests, "We followed up energetically."[433] For example, he said, Bruce Lindsey and Sandy Berger realized that certain documents had not been produced.[434] During the course of discussions with Berger and Lindsey, it became apparent that there were documents about whether President Clinton had authorized covert actions against Osama bin Laden[435] In response to this, a team of 9/11 Commission staff arranged to have an exhaustive document review at the National Archives.[436] For 18 hours, Zelikow and other Commission officials reviewed materials at the Archives.[437] This process, according to Zelikow, produced several important nuggets for the Commission's Final Report.[438] Zelikow used this anecdote to show that the Commission went to great lengths

---

[427] Dion Telephonic Interview.

[428] *Id..*

[429] *Id..*

[430] *Id..*

[431] *Id..*

[432] Zelikow Interview.

[433] *Id..*

[434] *Id..*

[435] *Id..*

[436] *Id..*

[437] *Id..*

[438] *Id..*

to ensure they had seen all responsive documents.[439] He said, "If we had any clue about something that was missing or incomplete, we hit it very hard."[440]

Zelikow said the Justice Department told them that Berger removed different versions of the Millennium Alert After Action Report, and based on these discussions the Commission believed this was the scope of the damage.[441] The Justice Department represented to Zelikow that they believed they had accounted for all the documents Berger had stolen.[442] The Department of Justice never advised Zelikow that Berger had access to original, uncopied materials.[443] If Zelikow had understood that there was a potential for Berger's actions to have gone beyond just the Millennium Report, it would have been a "grave concern."[444] If Zelikow had known Berger had such broad access to original documents, he would have wanted greater assurances from the Department of Justice that they had delimited the scope of Berger's removals and defined the extent of the damage to the document requests.[445]

In their book, Kean and Hamilton confirmed what Marcus said about the Commission relying on the Justice Department. On this subject they state:

> From our standpoint, the primary matter of concern was: Had we seen all of the documents we needed to see? The answer to that question was yes. The Justice Department assured us that copies of the documents in question had been sent by the Archives to the White House, and then made available to the Commission.[446]

When the Berger matter became public, Kean and Hamilton stated they had to explain to the media what the Department of Justice had assured them, "that the Commission had seen all of the documents Berger had removed because several copies had been made beforehand."[447]

---

[439] *Id.*.

[440] *Id.*.

[441] *Id.*.

[442] *Id.*.

[443] *Id.*.

[444] *Id.*.

[445] *Id.*.

[446] Kean & Hamilton at 183.

[447] *Id.*

It is now clear that this conclusion is limited only to those documents Berger was known to have taken. It does not reflect at all the very real possibility that he took other documents.

VII. Conclusion

The country may never know the full effect of Berger's misconduct. His deliberate calculating actions to remove highly classified documents compromised the national security of this country in more ways than one. His unauthorized removal of documents by itself is sanctioned by the criminal law, and he has been prosecuted. The temporary abandonment of highly classified documents at a construction site could have resulted in the disclosure of sensitive material to our enemies. That is why we protect classified documents and require that they be handled in very restricted circumstances.

Berger's misconduct took advantage of serious weaknesses in controls over classified documents, including weaknesses in the proper response to the discovery of the unauthorized removal of such documents. The failure to bring in law enforcement early in the process has left open questions about the scope of Berger's actions. Because he had access to original uninventoried documents during two of his visits, he was in a position to remove original documents without being detected. Early involvement of law enforcement might have found additional documents or might have given sound reasons for concluding that no other documents were taken. Instead, Berger was notified about the missing documents, and he pled guilty to the unauthorized removal of documents that he was caught removing even before law enforcement was notified.

Finally, in an era where information sharing is a critical watchword for preventing terrorist attacks, no one shared information with the 9/11 Commission regarding the full scope of Berger's possible misconduct. Indeed, the Justice Department's assurances to the 9/11 Commission and the public plainly suggested that the Department was able to conclude that Berger did not take other documents. The Justice Department did not know and could not have known whether Berger took other documents. Representations to the Commission and to the public were incomplete and misleading, preventing the public and the Commission from properly weighing and evaluating whether Berger's access to original documents could have influenced the Commission's findings.

Perhaps the 9/11 Commission would have concluded that Berger's access to original documents did not result in any additional missing documents and therefore had no impact on the Commission's work. But the Commission should have been put in a position to reach that conclusion on its own. But without timely disclosure to the 9/11 Commission of the complete facts surrounding Berger's misconduct, that question will unfortunately remain unanswered.

Colophon

This book was produced using Microsoft Word and Adobe Acrobat.

Heading fonts and the body text inside the book are in Palatino Linotype, chosen because it is a nimble-looking font. Quotations are in Courier. The American Heritage® Dictionary of the English Language, Fourth Edition, copyright © 2000 by Houghton Mifflin Company defines col·o·phon as follows:

> An ancient Greek city of Asia Minor northwest of Ephesus. It was famous for its cavalry.

Along the same lines, Webster's Revised Unabridged, copyright 1996, 1998, MICRA, Inc.:

> \Col"o*phon\ (k[o^]l"[-o]*f[o^]n), n. [L. colophon finishing stroke, Gr. kolofw`n; cf. L. culmen top, collis hill. Cf. Holm.] An inscription, monogram, or cipher, containing the place and date of publication, printer's name, etc., formerly placed on the last page of a book.

I always look for an appropriate and substantive "finishing stroke" to finish each book.   In this case, what better words could I suggest than ██████████████?